Acknowledgments

Thanks to Emma and Luke for all the joys and challenges that being your mother has brought to my life. I admire you for the brave young adults you have become.

Thanks to Mum and Dad for the many ways you have helped out over the years.

Thanks to my family and friends for your encouragement, prayers and support through all the tough years. Thanks also to Bruce and Fern, particularly for all your help with minding Luke when I needed to be with Emma in England for her assessments and operation. Thanks to many of the teachers and staff at Emma and Luke's school who went above and beyond the call of duty to be of help to our family unit in our time of crisis.

Thanks to the CF team who have given Emma and Luke fantastic care over the years. Dr Greally, Dr Basil, Ger Leen, Ger Clancy and Margaret Fitzsimmons, I wish we could have you as our team always. You are like a second family to us. Ger Leen, it has been very special to me that you joined the CF team the year Emma and Luke were diagnosed with CF. You have been through so much with us through the years. Thanks also to the rest of the team, lung function technicians, dieticians, physiotherapists, nurses on the wards and to everyone at the hospital who have been involved in Emma and Luke's care over the years.

Thanks to Mr Bhagwan for the past twenty years of encouragement and wisdom.

Thanks to the transplant team, nurses and staff at Newcastle for everything. Thank you to Peter and Eileen for welcoming us into your home and Church.

Thanks to Alan our minister and friend, I believe you were a God send because you arrived as minister of our church the summer before Emma's health deteriorated and over the years after that your pastoral care was second to none.

Thanks to Ronan who patiently listened to me and guided me through a tough season of my life.

Thanks to the team at Ambassador who have helped to make my dream about this book become a reality.

Contents

Introduction

For a long time now I have known that one day I would write a book. I hope that in sharing some of our difficult life's experiences with all who read it that it will encourage others to persevere through tough times.

I wasn't sure when to start writing. So in those days I decided I would keep an occasional journal of what I was going through and then I would have these notes when writing the book later. I knew when the time came to start writing because I was aware of chapters closing and my life moving forward.

I chose the title because our lives have been like riding a roller- coaster with all the ups and downs, crisis and challenges, good times and bad times. Sometimes life trundled along, challenging but manageable. Other times it turned into an extreme ride when crisis took over and all we could do was hold on tight and trust that God was in control.

For some of the chapters in this book, Emma and Luke contribute by writing about how things were from their perspective with regard to their health. They have been through a lot, particularly in the year when Emma was critically ill, so I think it is part of their healing to share what their thoughts were going through the tough times. When they share it's from the perspective of what they remember of that time. Although the three of us have lived with CF for nineteen years, we all have different experiences and perspectives of it. Emma can share what it is like for a young person to have CF and what it was like to cope with the awfulness particularly when her health became critical. Luke will have had a different, less intense, experience of CF but he also had the experience of seeing his sister critically ill, knowing he had the same illness and this could possibly be ahead for him one day too. I can share from my perspective of what it has been like, as their mother and carer, nursing them through almost twenty years of long term illness. I think it is interesting to see it from different perspectives.

One of the other reasons for writing this book is that I feel Cystic Fibrosis is a hidden illness. It's human nature for people to think that what they see is how things are. However with CF, the sufferer can so look well on the outside but inside is a different story. It's a daily battle to maintain their health.

One of the aims of the book is to raise the awareness of the silent suffering that people with CF, and their carers, have to cope with during their lives. While every CF sufferer and carer will identify with parts of our story, their experience will also be different as there are so many forms and progressions of the illness. Also they will be at different stages of their journey of living with CF.

The book is also a celebration of the support and encouragement we have had from family and friends over the years and an acknowledgment of the special people we have met along the way. I have not mentioned everyone by name because I'm likely to leave someone out and I don't want to upset anyone. I think most people will recognise themselves in the book anyway.

Whenever I read a book that I enjoy or that impacts me, I try to contact the author to encourage and thank them. If this is true for you too, and you would like to contact me, my email is lifeonrollercoaster@hotmail.com

Although our story is intense at times, I hope you will find it inspiring and encouraging too.

Helen

1

The Journey Begins

Emma's secondary school form teacher asked the teenage students what they would like to be when they grew up. There was the usual answers of chosen careers and also some who had no idea what they would like to do with their lives. When it came to Emma's turn to answer, she said she would like to be alive. The teacher was jolted by this reply but Emma was just being honest. She had been born with a terminal illness and at the time that she answered this question her health was deteriorating and her future was uncertain. That was in 2003 but little did we know what was ahead for us in the next three years.

Let's go back to the beginning of the story that had brought us to this point.

Shortly after my first wedding anniversary, my daughter Emma was born. I had been looking forward to her arrival and to the experience of being a mother, nurturing her as she developed and grew through the different phases of childhood. I'll never forget the moment of her birth when the doctor held her up so I could see her. He said "What have you got?" I could barely answer his question because I was choked with emotion as I looked at my beautiful daughter. All the wards were full so I had to wait in the labour ward until a bed became available in the main ward. While I was waiting I asked a nurse if she would lift Emma on to my bed so I could talk to her. Although the nurse was reluctant to do this at first, as I was still numb from the epidural, we agreed that if Emma was lying between me and the wall there would be no chance of her falling off the bed.

As I held Emma close to me, I welcomed her to the world and talked to her about the family she had been born into and our life. It was a very special moment and even though it was many years ago now, I can still remember it as if it happened yesterday. It was one of my life's defining moments.

After the birth, the next couple of months passed by all too quickly as we settled into the new routine that comes with having a baby. I thought she was the most beautiful baby. She was petite and had beautiful blue eyes that always seemed to be so alert. She was full of smiles. Whenever we were out and about people would stop to talk to us because of Emma's smiles and energy.

In November when my maternity leave was over, I had to go back to work. I didn't want to. I wanted to stay at home with her because those early days are special days. Even though the baby days are lots of hard work, they pass by quickly and you can never get them back. I wanted to be there to see every little milestone. As with a lot of young married couples we needed the finances so I reluctantly returned to working outside the home.

My husband had taken that first week off to mind Emma and on my first morning back to work, he phoned to say that Emma had been coughing so he brought her to our doctor.

The doctor diagnosed a chest infection and also sent Emma with her Dad to the children's hospital for an x-ray. The hospital said she was a baby who had lots of mucus and they recommended physiotherapy. I felt none of this was a good sign.

Emma was quite small so to do the physiotherapy at home I would put a pillow across my lap and lie her on top of it. Then I would gently tap her chest or back with two fingers, the way we had been told to do. Most times she did not mind the physiotherapy and sometimes the motion of gentle tapping would send her asleep.

A month later, on my Christmas Eve birthday, Emma was unwell again. We brought her back to our family doctor and he sent us to the same hospital for an x-ray as Emma had another chest infection. The result of the hospital visit was a recommendation to increase the physiotherapy we were doing daily to help clear the mucus from her lungs. By now she was almost four months old but was already on her second course of antibiotics to clear up chest infections. In hindsight, there were other symptoms as well. Although she was a happy baby and was reaching her developmental milestones, she was not thriving physically. She had a chesty cough. Her feeds didn't satisfy her. She would be hungry after three hours. Many times when we would burp her to bring up the wind after her feed, a lot of the milk would come back out of her mouth in a projectile fountain. It was exhausting night after night not to be getting much sleep because she was awake every three hours or so needing food and then not settling back to sleep. She was my first baby so I had no experience of motherhood to compare this with. Many months later an uncle of mine told me that when he saw Emma that Christmas he thought she would not live until the New Year because she looked so unwell.

The following March, when Emma was seven months old, I thought I was pregnant again and I made an appointment with our family doctor to have this confirmed. The baby would be due in October, so there would only be thirteen months between Emma and her baby brother or sister. I had forgotten to bring my cheque book with me to pay for the visit to the doctor so I had to return that evening to settle my account. I brought Emma with me and the GP was very concerned that he could hear Emma's noisy breathing when he was on the far side of two closed doors and we were in the waiting room. I was also very concerned that there had been no improvement in Emma's breathing since we had started the physiotherapy on her. He decided to refer Emma to a Consultant friend of his who would check further into her breathing difficulties.

At our first appointment the Consultant thought that Emma might be allergic to milk so he took her off all milk products and put her on soya. A chest x-ray was done and it showed that Emma almost had pneumonia. These were very scary and frustrating days. She didn't look that bad on the outside but inside, her lungs were a different story. The change to soya made no difference so with that ticked off the list of probable causes the next step was to send her for sweat tests. I prayed about the tests that Emma was to have and the day before the first of a series of three sweat tests in the hospital, I was at home listening to the radio. The presenter was talking to a young girl with Cystic Fibrosis who had had a transplant and in the course of the interview she mentioned the sweat tests which had been done initially to determine if she had CF or not. I got such a shock and as I listened to the interview I cried and cried. What was this illness? How would we cope if our beautiful, happy baby had it? What would the future hold for her? What quality of life would she have? How serious was the illness? Was she going to die from it? Was transplant ahead for her too? So many 'what if' questions were racing through my mind. I had to try to put those questions aside and concentrate on getting us through the next step which was the sweat tests.

For these tests, a solution was rubbed on both sides of her arm until a slightly red reaction appeared. Pads were placed on either side of her arms with wires leading to a black box. A slight electric current was switched on for about five minutes and then the current was gradually switched off. The test did not hurt, she would just have felt a slight tingling sensation in her arm. A small circular cotton pad was taped to her arm for half an hour so her sweat could be collected on the pad. Later the cotton pad was weighed to see if there was enough sweat for the test. What they were looking for was the amount of salt in the sweat because people with Cystic Fibrosis have a higher salt content in their sweat. I had noticed before at times when Emma was a baby that I could taste salt when I kissed her face after she had been crying. Emma was so good for the test, she sat quietly on my lap and did not seem to mind the test being done. She was equally good for the second test six days later. On the day of the final test we had an appointment to see the Consultant to hear the results of the previous tests. I was stunned to hear the Consultant's words confirming that she had CF.

We had so many questions that we needed answered. The Consultant answered most of the questions but some of them couldn't be answered such as 'How long will she live?' because at that early stage it was impossible to tell. It was devastating to hear that Emma had such a serious illness but at the same time it was a relief that after all these months of not knowing why she wasn't thriving that there was a name for her condition and help in the form of medication and treatment.

After the doctor had told us that Emma had CF we were brought into an adjoining room where the Consultant examined her. I was eighteen weeks pregnant with my next baby and, in a way, hearing about Emma's CF at this point took the decision about planning to have another baby out of my hands. In the sense that it would be harder to plan a pregnancy now knowing the risks involved. I tried to put it out of my mind that the baby might have CF, after all, there was nothing I could do to change the outcome. So for the duration of the pregnancy I put my energy into looking after Emma and nursing her in her new healthcare routine.

There were many different reactions to people hearing that Emma had such a serious illness. Some people were just as stunned as we had initially been when they heard about Emma's illness. Mostly people were supportive and encouraging to us. One or two people suggested that Emma may grow out of her CF in a year but we knew that was not likely.

One positive thing we noticed from early on is that they always seemed to be making advances in the areas of research, care and treatment of Cystic Fibrosis. As CF is an inherited disease it amazed me that it had not shown up in either of the families so far.

Here comes the gene therapy bit that may sound confusing but that's only because the possibilities with each birth are so random.

- In order to have a child with CF, both parents have to be carriers of the CF gene.

- Every time I would become pregnant, there would be a one in four chance that I would have a child with CF.

- Or a two in four chance I could have a child who does not have the illness but is a carrier of the CF gene.

- Or a one in four chance I could have a child who does not have the illness and is not a carrier.

- If only one parent is the carrier then they could not have a child with CF but they could pass on the CF gene so the child would be a carrier.

- Or they may not pass on the gene and so the child would not be a carrier.

Amazingly, when the research team later looked into the family tree they discovered that both of my parents were carriers. So going by the statistics there was the potential that they could have had one child with CF. Instead, they had four children and none of us had CF but three of us are carriers. We would never have known this except for Emma having been diagnosed with CF because there are no symptoms if you are only a carrier of the illness. About one in 20 of the population in Ireland are carriers.

In a person with CF their body produces a thick and sticky mucus which clogs up the airways and also causes problems in the digestive system. As Emma almost had pneumonia by the time she was diagnosed, the doctor needed to monitor her progress.

In these early days, we attended the clinic more regularly just until her medication regime was established. Names of her medications, antibiotics and enzymes all became a familiar part of everyday life for us. Almost immediately she started to put on weight, sleep better (at last) and she began to thrive. She needed daily physiotherapy to help loosen the mucus and clear it from the lungs to prevent a build up of mucus that could become infected. If she got a chest infection she would need antibiotics to clear it and each chest infection would leave scarring on the lungs, which in turn would leave the lungs weaker for fighting the next infection. We continued with Emma's physiotherapy. It was the most disliked part of her treatment even at this young age. At times, when she would not co-operate with the physiotherapy, I tried to make it into a game.

Another major part of her condition was that the natural enzymes in her digestive system were blocked because of the mucus so she would need to take enzyme capsules with all her food that contains fat to help break down the fat content. As she was still quite young she would not be able to swallow the capsules whole so I would open the capsules and put the granules on a mouthful of her food or yogurt. This made it easier for her to swallow them.

There was so much to take on board regarding her new healthcare but I was relieved that she was getting the help she needed and I was determined to learn as much about her illness so I could nurse her to the best of my abilities.

A few times when I thought about it, I was more than a little ticked off with life's unfairness. I never drank or smoked, I ate a healthy diet and kept reasonably fit. Yet Emma was born with a terminal illness because of this recessive gene that I hadn't even known I was carrying. It is only natural at times like that to wonder why do things like this happen in life. Apparently it is normal to wonder if this was some type of punishment but as I did not have the energy to waste on negative thoughts I just put our circumstances down to the fact that it's the consequences of living in a broken world. I tried to look at the positives instead, we had a beautiful baby whose smiles, alertness and personality brought so much to our lives. I loved being her mother and determined that I would be the best mother in the world to her. In the moment that I was told Emma had CF I decided that we would live as normal a life as possible within the confines of her illness. With all the advances in care and treatment for people with CF, it meant that she could live well into her thirties or longer so it was important for her to have as much normality as possible. It was a huge responsibility to be nursing a child with such a serious illness as CF but I trusted we would get though all of this with the help of God. I think in those days my faith in God was simple but strong. I didn't know just how much it was to deepen over the next number of years through times of adversity.

I am the kind of person who copes better with being prepared and knowing as much as possible about any given situation I'm going through. For me, it gives a kind of security because there's less chance of events taking me by surprise. So I decided I would find out as much as possible about Emma's illness. Although they were working on a cure, at this point in time it was still a terminal illness. I put that piece of knowledge to the back of my mind, it was for some future time and to think too much about that now would rob me of the strength to face each day in the present. The illness gets progressively worse over time but for the moment we were in a reasonably good phase. By that I mean that she was well enough to be nursed at home and had responded well to the medication so far.

Over time, caring for Emma in her illness has changed me and I suppose the first thing I learned was to live in the moment, enjoy the good times because they strengthen you and help you to cope better with the bad times.

We continued with the medications and physiotherapy regime and looked forward to the birth of a baby brother or sister for Emma.

In mid October, Emma's baby brother was born. I had always said after my previous experience of giving birth, that if I were to go through it again I would ask for the epidural as soon as I reached the hospital. However his birth was so quick I had no time to ask for pain relief and if I had delayed getting to the hospital that day, it would have been a home birth. I had always had the name Mark in my mind but when I saw him I knew his name was Luke.

Luke's first few weeks were different to how Emma had been as a baby. He kept his milk down and didn't regurgitate his feeds back in a projectile fountain. He slept contently, in fact he slept so well and so quietly that often I would have to go up really close to him to check if he was still breathing. I tried not to think about the sweat tests he would have to have when he was six weeks old.

Time went by quick enough and before we knew it the morning of the first of three sweat tests had arrived. I can still picture him that morning. He was propped up against the cushions on the couch in our living room, dressed in a little outfit my parents had given him as a present. I was sitting close to him chatting to him about the hospital and what they would do. As he was only a baby he would not understand what I was saying to him but he responded to the soft tones of my voice and he gurgled and gooed as if he was trying to talk back to me. He was always such a sociable baby. That was another defining moment in my life, 18 years later I can still picture it.

He had a sweat test on three different mornings and then at a meeting with the Consultant it was confirmed that Luke also had CF. Initially I was stunned. His health seemed so different to Emma's. He didn't have the chesty cough. He was thriving. He hadn't had the same health issues Emma had when she had been his age. There are so many different forms of the illness, maybe his was a milder form. Or maybe it was just that it was discovered earlier so he didn't have the early chest infections that Emma had.

The Consultant discussed the antibiotics, medicines and enzymes that Luke would be started on and we also had to do the physiotherapy with him. We knew the drill at this stage. I got through listening about the information to do with Luke's regime but outside the Consultant's office later, when I was putting Luke's coat on, all the emotions of hearing the diagnosis caught up with me and I started crying. Luke was so small in my arms I wished I could protect him and Emma from this awful illness and all that it would mean for their lives and yet I knew I couldn't, it was out of my hands. In that moment I determined that I would nurse them to the best of my abilities and be there for them through every step of their illness. In some ways, the fact that they both had CF meant that Emma and Luke would be good company and comfort for each other as they would understand what the other was going through. In other ways it just added more uncertainty to the future as we did not know how the illness would develop in them. At this early stage there was no way of knowing how long they would live for and what quality of life they would have, we just had to take a day at a time.

In their early years, their health were reasonable so long as we kept up the regular regime of daily medication, physiotherapy and nebulisers. I discovered early on that living with a long term illness like CF is not just a few bits and pieces of treatment that are done each day. It is a lifestyle. I also discovered that normality of family life for us included a lot of extra responsibility and nursing that would not be included in what others define as normality for their family lives. I did the best I could each day and encouraged the children to live as active a life as possible. We had regular clinic visits so the doctors and CF team could monitor their progress. Emma and Luke always complied with taking their medicine or enzymes with all their food. To them it was normal, they had never known anything different. Their illness didn't stop us from going out, we just brought the necessary medicine with us. If they went to a party, they knew how important it was to take extra enzymes with the party food as this type of food is more likely to have extra fat in it. I would always explain things to them in an age appropriate way that they could understand. For example, when they were little, I explained the importance of taking their enzymes by telling them that if they didn't do that they could get a pain in their stomach. If their friends asked what the capsules were, they would give them the same explanation and their friends just accepted that explanation as young children do.

The thing with it being a progressive illness is that you grow into it, in the sense that every so often more medication or a new treatment is added to their routine. It would be too overwhelming if we had to take it on board all at once. When Emma was four and Luke was three, they both began using nebulisers twice a day. The solution has to be prepared and is then put into the nebuliser. When the compressor is switched on, the vapour goes down onto their lungs and helps to deal with infections. The practicalities of this being added to their routine was that the nebulised medication had to be done every day regardless of whatever else we were doing. If we were going out anywhere like visiting family or friends, we had to bring the nebuliser and medication with us. If we waited till we came home we would all be in bed late because the nebs had to be done. Missing the odd dose now and then would not do any harm but it was most effective if kept in a routine with no doses missed. As they got older and started school, I noticed at times like summer holidays from school that if we were getting up later and the nebulisers were given at a later time in the morning, that their coughs got worse. So I made the decision every morning of the school holidays to get up early, mix up the solution for both of their nebulisers and bring it up to their bedrooms. This way they could stay in their warm beds for their morning dose of medicine and afterwards they could have a lie-in. The nebuliser would take about 10-15 minutes and they would sit upright for this. I would also give them their oral medication at this time to keep it in the same routine as the school term time for the sake of their health. At this stage they also had reviews at the hospital every three months and an Annual Assessment once a year.

Before Luke was born, the Company I had been working for had transferred their business back to Scotland and I was made redundant. I didn't look for another job because there was a lot involved in Emma and Luke's healthcare and I needed to be at home nursing them.

I found that there was a certain amount of information available about CF and although I read up on it, most of the knowledge came from my experience of nursing Emma and Luke.

Life was challenging in those early days as we combined the Cystic Fibrosis medication and treatment regime into our daily routine along with the usual everyday demands of the busyness of family life with young children. It wasn't all doom and gloom and we had many happy times together enjoying normal family activities and Emma and Luke's fun loving personalities. I realized that when living with a long term illness there are no promises of tomorrow so we tried to enjoy the good moments to the fullest and in doing so would build happy memories that would sustain us through the difficult days.

Although we had plenty of health challenges to contend with every day, our daily routine was reasonably manageable at this point in the sense that neither of the children needed to be in hospital and most of the time they kept well so long as the daily medication regime was administered.

It seems sometimes in life that so many challenges come together. I didn't know it at the time but I was shortly going to experience another difficult time.

2

Worst Wilderness Experience

Over the period of a few years my marriage broke down irretrievably. The only way forward was to separate which was not a decision I came to lightly.

These were very stressful times and somewhere in the middle of all this I plummeted into the darkest, blackest pit I have ever experienced in my life.

I had been getting through all the challenges I was facing moment by moment and trusting God for His help but then something triggered off a huge volcano of pain that had been hidden inside me and my life came crashing down before me. I couldn't see any way forward at that time. Looking back now, I can see that part of the problem was that over years I had bottled up things instead of dealing with each issue at the time. So when any new issue came along it was heaped on top of old issues and it compounded the present issue making it harder to deal with. It sounds simple when put into a few sentences but it took me years to realise this. I struggled with the future we were facing and I knew my only hope was to cry out to God for His mercy and help. I just wanted to stay under my duvet cover in a darkened room and sleep. I didn't want to face life, it was too difficult. It was a chore to force myself out of bed in the morning, I only did it for the children because I knew they needed me. However, as soon as I had given them breakfast, sorted their medicines and nebulisers, and brought them to school I would go home and get back into bed. I would set my alarm clock and sleep in bed until the horrible noise of the alarm clock woke me from my place of safety and warmth where there were no responsibilities.

My faith had always helped me to look beyond difficult circumstances and given me hope but now I had lost my focus and was overwhelmed with so many difficulties happening at once. I felt stripped of hope so it was difficult to be motivated to do anything in the present to improve my situation.

The previous year a minister friend of mine who knew my situation, regarding the children's illness and the marriage breakdown, had recommended a counsellor friend of his just in case I needed someone neutral to talk to. At the time I didn't need to see a counsellor but a year later it was a different story with all these major stressful things coming together. Although I had good friends who willingly listened for hours about different aspects of what I was going through, I felt it would be better to talk to one neutral person about everything I was going through. I plucked up the courage to pick up the phone to make an appointment to see the counsellor knowing there might be a waiting list. I would not have minded waiting, it was going to take courage to look into the problems in my life and to sort through them, I wasn't sure that I could be that strong.

However when the counsellor heard all that I was going through he gave me an appointment for the following week. He was very easy to talk to and over the next while we worked through the issues and problems that had built up over time. Sometimes there were baby steps and sometimes there were giant leaps forward. Talking through the issues gave me a clearer head to think about what, if any, steps I needed to improve a situation and move forward with my life. At some later point, I realized that I didn't need to see him anymore for counselling. He said that affirmed to him that his job was complete and we both knew it was time for me to move on. Each Christmas the children and I would visit him to keep in contact with him as he had been a key person in my life helping me to move forward with life when I had become stuck.

My relationship with God was an important part of my life as far back as 12 years old and I would say that since then I had a strong faith in God. I was now moving into a deeper, relationship with Him as I faced challenges that meant I had to put my faith into practice and learn to trust more.

One of the things I love about God is that He meets us wherever we are. Every day I prayed that He would give me strength to get through the day. In the middle of all the awfulness I discovered the power of encouragement and perseverance. I read many books about people in history who persevered and did not give up even though the odds were stacked against them. Eventually their perseverance paid off and they were successful in achieving their goals.

George Adams once said that encouragement is like oxygen to the soul, without it we die but with it we can overcome great obstacles. I would often think about the truth of that sentence and let it sink into my being. I was going through one of the worst times in my life and needed plenty of encouragement, personally and spiritually. I couldn't remember all the encouragement coming my way because there was so much so I decided to start two different 'Encouragement Books' - one personal and one spiritual. I would write down encouraging words in these books so that when I was feeling sad and deflated I could read these words which would lift my spirit.

My personal 'Encouragement Book' was an ordinary lined, hard backed book with a picture cover on it. In the column at the left-hand side I would write the date. On the line next to that I would write the encouraging words that someone had said to me.

This is what a page in the book would have looked like...

10.01.96 (A friend whom I have great admiration for) said I would definitely be in her life raft and she would be taking instructions from me.

18.04. 96 (Our pharmacist and friend), introduced me to a new member of staff and told them I am a phenomenal person.

20.08.96 My solicitor, on hearing about Emma and Luke's home IV's, said he thinks I am marvelous.

In my spiritual 'Encouragement Book' I would write whatever it was that day that strengthened me, encouraged me not to give up and had helpful advice for taking the next step forward or persevering. This encouragement came from many different places, the Bible, daily Bible notes, encouraging words in poems or on cards, emails, phone calls, Christian books, TV programmes, a sentence from a sermon, women's conferences, reading about difficulties in other people's lives (Bible times, history, modern times) and seeing how God transformed their lives, brought healing and move them towards their goals.

I had so many fears at this time in my life but now I was in a situation where circumstances which were not of my choosing were forcing me to face all of those fears. I didn't really appreciate having to persevere in facing them but years later I would look back and see how this had changed me and made me stronger. I learnt that to think too far into the future robbed me of the strength to live today. All we are guaranteed is this moment in time.

It took many years but I finally came to a point where I didn't think I was 'just surviving' anymore, I felt as if I had turned a corner and 1 knew no matter what happened in the future I would never ever be back in that awful hopelessness again. I had learnt practical lessons that would stand to me for coping with life's difficult times. Things like setting myself a realistic goal every day of completing two or three priorities for that day instead of feeling overwhelmed by all the things that were crowding in on top of me. Also daily choosing to concentrate more on the positives than the negatives. If I was feeling down I had learnt practicalities like not staying indoors but going out for a walk or meeting a friend for coffee. I learnt about doing whatever I could do to take control of my circumstances rather than them controling me.

My relationship with God had reached new heights. He never gave up on me even when I had given up on myself. I went into that phase of my life with low self-esteem and very little sense of who I was or where I was going in life. It was a time of self discovery and maturing and I came out the far side of this challenging time having proved God as my Prince of Peace (through trusting Him in trying circumstances), my Counselor (in helping me to sort through problems), my Helper (in time of need), my Friend (who was always with me), my Shepherd (who looked after me and guided me), my Guide (who led me every step of the way) , my Redeemer, Mighty One, Faithful One, my Refuge from the storm, my Deliverer, my Shield, my Stronghold in the Day of Trouble.

3

Living With CF

Over the years, people have often said I play down the demands of our situation but I think it's just that I'm a survivor. I would try to focus on what the priorities were for any given day regarding their health needs and our survival. If there was time for anything after that, good, but if not then the things that didn't get done would have to wait for another day. I was determined that the children would have as normal a life as possible. Although CF is a terminal illness as there is no cure for it at the moment, they are working on finding a cure and regularly have new treatments available to improve the life of the person with this condition. Before I had children, when I thought of what I would like family life to be like, I hoped for an active outdoor family life with lots of walking, cycling and sports.

CF curtailed these hopes and plans but we still managed to have a reasonably active life.

In their pre teen years Emma and Luke were involved in the usual childhood activities. They often won awards for their achievements, participation in activities and for 100% attendance at these activities. I often told them that to get an award for 100% attendance was like a double achievement as they had often overcome health issues to be given such an award.

Living with a long term illness affects all aspects of life. There were daily treatments to be done at this pre teen stage of the illness. There was physiotherapy, nebulisers two to three times a day, oral medication two to three times a day and enzymes that had to be taken with all food containing fat, which is basically all food except vegetables and fruit.

When they were babies I opened the capsule granules onto a spoonful of yogurt to help them swallow the enzymes easier. Then when they were a few years old they were able to swallow the capsules whole. People with CF often have problems putting on weight or keeping it on. This in turn leads to problems with fighting infections. They can need up to 50% more calories than other children of their age so this requires extra daily snacks plus the more expensive cuts of meat to get the most from their food. It was a constant challenge to be thinking of interesting and appetizing snacks to help keep the weight on. To put our weekly food bill in context, a friend said she would only spend our weekly total if she were catering for a small group.

Sometimes it felt like a losing battle because although they ate a good variety of food they were still on the lower percentile lines on the weight chart. If they got an infection and didn't feel like eating much, they would lose weight. When the infection had cleared we would have the challenge again of trying to increase their weight to get them further up the weight chart. The dietician from our CF team was always available to give helpful advice about practical ways to increase calories. However, the main problem was trying to find practical ways to encourage them to eat extra food when they didn't feel like doing so, particularly if they were going through a time of being unwell. Emma and Luke were also encouraged to take high calorie shakes to increase their daily calorie intake. At every meal Emma and Luke would ask me how many enzymes they needed to take with the food they were eating. I would try to calculate in my mind a rough idea of how much fat I thought was in the meal and then calculate the amount of enzymes they would need.

As they got a bit older, I taught them how to look at the nutritional label on the back of food or snacks they were eating to find out how much fat was in it. Then they would be able to calculate the amount of enzymes they should take with it. They were living with a lifetime illness so they would need to be able to calculate the enzymes for times when they were out somewhere without me so they could be more independent as they got older. The amount of enzymes depended on the fat content of what was being eaten. It was best if the enzymes were taken at regular intervals throughout the meal to give their system the best chance of digesting the food.

I found in their early childhood years when I got the rare chance to go out for a meal with friends I would check my handbag to see if I had the enzymes, even though the children were at home with the babysitter. That's just part of living with long term illness. It invades every area of your life. There is no break from it. It becomes part of you, whether you are the person who has the illness or you are the carer.

The daily physiotherapy was essential as it helped to clear the mucus from the lungs. The type of physiotherapy depended on their age. Initially when they were very young I would lie them over a pillow or cushion which was on my lap. Then I would clap the front, back and sides of their chest with my cupped hand. The cupped hand creates an air pocket so the clapping does not hurt them but it releases the mucus on their lungs enabling them to cough it up. This physiotherapy would take 10-15 minutes every day for each of them. A physiotherapist who called to our house from the CF Association gave us a half dome shaped piece of foam. At separate times, Emma and Luke would lie over it in one of the postural drainage positions. I could then clap their chest to help release the mucus. As they grew older they were taught to do the clapping exercises on themselves. They never really took to that, so I did the physiotherapy every day on them.

Sometimes my upper arms ached with the 20-30 minutes of constant clapping for their daily physiotherapy. It was quite demanding to fit it in with all the other things we had to do. Luke always seemed to have a milder form of CF and had the energy to keep active.

I don't remember him giving out about having the physiotherapy. It was different for Emma. She always detested the daily session of physiotherapy so it was a challenge to get this done. Later on when they were older a physiotherapy device would be introduced which encouraged them to take responsibility for their own daily physiotherapy regimes.

Another major part of the daily routine was the oral medications and nebulisers. I set aside part of a kitchen cupboard for these medicines. I had a list inside the cupboard door which detailed their medications, dosage and daily times these should be taken. There was one column for Emma and one for Luke as they were not always on exactly the same treatments. I found the list necessary so I could keep track of their medicines. The dosage varied for each tablet Some were daily, some twice daily, some three times daily, some weekly or alternate days. At times the routine was more complicated with three antibiotics being rotated every two weeks. At other times they would be on a reducing amount of steroids over a period of time. They had regular blood tests at their clinic visits and we were contacted by the team at the hospital when medications needed to be changed. I had a weekly list of medicines to collect from the chemist to see us through the following week.

Emma and Luke also had nebulisers to take every day. One in the morning and evening which had to be prepared just before the dose was nebulised. There was a different nebuliser at lunchtime for which the medicine came already prepared. We just had to snap off the top of the vial and put the liquid into the nebuliser. They would breathe this in over ten to fifteen minutes.

The nebuliser had to be taken apart and washed after each session. It was then left to dry on a paper towel. Each week the nebuliser parts were to be given an extra cleaning in boiling water.

The nebulisers were serviced once a year which involved me delivering them to the Oxygen company in the local industrial estate. They would service them that day and I could collect them in the afternoon.

Added to the daily treatments were the check ups every three months which included height and weight checks, oxygen saturation check and pulmonary function test to see how the lungs were performing. A cough swab would also be taken and sent to the laboratory to see if there was any infection present that needed treatment with an antibiotic. The clinic visit would also include a visit to the consultant and the nurse specialist. This whole visit would take up a morning at the hospital.

Added to the daily treatment and the regular check ups was the Annual Assessment. This included an x-ray, blood tests, physiotherapy , height and weight checks, blood pressure, skin folds check (in the early years), urine sample and cough swab/sputum sample.

There were also visits to the dietician, physiotherapist, Consultant and nurse specialist. A couple of weeks before the annual assessment we had to fill in a five day food diary of everything that Emma and Luke ate detailing quantities and the type of food or drink taken. The dietician would analyse this to see if they were getting all the calories and vitamins that they needed. As they got older a glucose tolerance test was included in the Annual Assessment as a certain percentage of CF sufferers also develop diabetes. The earlier diabetes is detected the quicker the treatment can be started. The Glucose Tolerance Test involved fasting from midnight. In the morning before going to the hospital I would put the numbing cream on their hand or arm so that by the time it came for the blood tests, they would be less painful. After the first blood test they would be given a drink of Lucozade appropriate to their weight. Then bloods would be taken every half hour for the next two and a half hours to see how the body was coping with the glucose in its system.

Sometimes an ultrasound scan was included in the annual assessment to check their kidneys.

There was also the emotional and psychological support needed to guide them through their illness. I always encouraged them to talk openly and not bottle it up inside. If they talked openly about it we could discuss it together. As they grew older, they became more aware of their illness and had questions that needed to be talked through with sensitivity and honesty appropriate to their age and understanding.

In their pre teen phase they had less independence than friends of their age who were beginning to enjoy weekends away with the youth club, summer camps or Easter camps.

If Emma and Luke wanted to go on these weekends they would have to take on the responsibility for their medication and nebulisers or we would need to know there was a helper there who would be willing to take on the responsibility of helping them with their medication regime.

There were always extras to be done as well such as the yearly flu vaccine. One year I had had three or four bouts of tonsillitis and the doctor suggested that to keep me free from the flu I should have the vaccine too. I needed to be in my best health to look after Emma and Luke. It seemed a bit strange that after all the years of encouraging them through blood tests and flu vaccines that the situation was now reversed and I was now the one being encouraged to be brave for my flu vaccine.

Another part of their care was to watch out for was coughs and colds to make sure they didn't develop into a chest infection. If we were going to visit anyone we would have to know beforehand if anyone in the house was unwell with a cold. A non CF person would not be at risk from a CF infection but if the other person passed an infection to Emma and Luke it could have an adverse effect on them. Also I felt it was best if they were driven by car to school as they could not be expected to travel by bus having to deal with waiting in cold weather at bus stops or having coughing fits bringing up mucus when on the bus.

In the hospital clinics they separate people with different CF infections to minimise the risk of cross infection. Emma and Luke both had different CF infections but it was impossible to separate them as they live in the same house so we just had to be more careful that they didn't pass infections to each other. This meant keeping the house as clean as possible and them not sharing things like cutlery, glasses or towels.

Some of the antibiotics made them over sensitive to the sun so it was important to make sure they had a high factor sunscreen on to avoid sunburn.

As people with CF sweat more than usual, it was important for them to have clothes with a high cotton content.

Although I had no formal nurse training, I became a full time nurse to Emma and Luke though the necessity of the daily care they needed for their CF.

Sometimes when I look back, I'm amazed that we were able to do much normal living. One of the things I learnt very early on is that life keeps going. I was aware that weeks and years would pass us by if we didn't try to include as much normality as possible in our routine.

Obviously there were times when the care of their CF took over but at those times we just had to pace ourselves to get through the ordeal believing that it wouldn't always be like that.

Regular socializing with friends was affected as anything that was planned may have to be cancelled at a moment's notice if we had to deal with a health issue. Sometimes I was just too exhausted to think about anything else but our immediate needs of basic living and the extra health issues we were living with. There were always bigger issues in the back of my mind that would have to wait for another time. I learned how to be thrifty and budget every penny that came in.

There was a certain satisfaction in knowing that I was spending wisely whatever money we had but there was always a huge fear that some unexpected bill would come in and we would not have the money to pay for it. There were also worries about their health and how it would affect them in the future. I was aware that I was juggling so many responsibilities and under a lot of stress. If my health failed we would be in a more desperate situation.

It was in those days that I learned complete reliance on God to provide completely for our needs and He never let us down.

When I asked Emma what she remembers about the primary school years, this is what she said…

To be honest at this stage I still didn't have much responsibility for my medicines and I kept reasonably well which meant I could enjoy life. I wasn't the one thinking about my medicine routine. Mum was the one having to think ahead. I was able to live my life knowing that my CF life and treatment was safe in Mum's (and the doctors) hands. Having to take enzymes with all my food wasn't really a bother either. As I was young, Mum was either there or she gave the enzymes to the adult in charge (If I was going to be out without Mum, she used to write the amount of enzymes I was to take with certain foods on the side of the enzyme container and I had an idea myself so it was all good). I suppose the fact that Mum tried to give us a normal life as possible and not wrap us up in cotton wool had something to do with the fact that it made CF more bearable to live with. It was the easier part of my CF life, as far as I'm concerned. I wasn't that sick. I could still do what all the other kids my age were doing, like sports and going to parties. I was growing physically and mentally at the same pace as the kids my age too. I felt like a normal child, 90% of the time. CF didn't stop me from doing the usual childhood things.
In school, the other children didn't really say much about me taking my enzymes. When they did asked I told them what they were for and I'd answer any questions they had as best as I could. I think it was half way through my primary school years quite a few people had already asked me and people who had asked me before were starting to ask me a second time. So I came up with a one

liner of what CF was in a nut shell and what the enzymes were for. Typically, people stopped asking me questions then. I'm not saying having CF was easy, there were plus and minus's. Physiotherapy was a drag because it took up so much time when I could have been playing with the other children and having fun. Nebulizers were ok cause they didn't take as long as physio but if they had said to me I didn't have to do them any more I wouldn't have been crying.

The one plus, at that stage, was being told I should have up to 50% more calories, to keep weight on so I could fight off infections. Like what child doesn't like to hear they can snack on chocolate bars (obviously with a balanced diet).

I asked Luke what he remembers of his CF in the pre teen years and this is what he said…

I didn't like having to do extra medicines and treatments. I had to get up early to do nebulisers and some other medicines. Then in the afternoon or at night I would have to come in early, from playing with my friends to do nebulisers. I also had to take enzymes every time I ate. I would always wait till no one was looking and then I would take them.

No one really said anything to me about it. I didn't like taking the enzymes. I knew I was different to other children but I didn't think about it because I was able to run around with everyone and play sports.

I didn't mind going to the hospital for annual assessments or for regular check ups because I was so used to it and all the staff were so nice there. It did help a bit that we talked about our Cystic Fibrosis openly between Mum, Emma and I but I never really thought about it to be honest. The way I deal with things is that if I don't think about it often it doesn't affect me but when I do I know that there are people in my family, friends or the church that I can talk to.

With Cystic Fibrosis you have to do physiotherapy and have to eat up to 50% more calories than children without CF. I thought that it was great because it meant I got to eat chocolate and crisps. Sometimes its hard to make the effort to eat if you don't feel well and it's harder to put on the weight then. I didn't really mind the physio at the start because I didn't need much as I was so active. As you get older you have to do more physio and that's when I found it more annoying.

I'm very aware that the intensity of our story is hard for people to digest at times and whenever I'm talking about our journey with CF I always try to say a mixture of the reality of living with CF but also some of the positive things in our life because of Emma and Luke's CF. One of those positive things is some of the people we have met along the way, like our pharmacist. Over the years, his positive and encouraging comments, which are grounded in practical wisdom, have been such a blessing to us. He, and all of his staff, have been a very important and special part of our lives. Many times I have written in my 'Encouragement book' kind, positive and encouraging comments that they have said to us.

Another positive is the great support over the years from family, friends, our Church and the schools which Emma and Luke attended. They have listened, encouraged, prayed and also supported our fund raising endeavors many times.

One of our special memories goes back to the time when Emma and Luke were 6 and 5 years old respectively. They were given the chance of a lifetime. Their CF Nurse Specialist, Ger, who had joined the team at the hospital in the year Emma and Luke were diagnosed with CF, gave me some information about a trip to Lapland with the hospital.

United Travel had organized a trip for 90 children, 10 nurses and 2 doctors to go to Lapland. My initial reaction was to allow them to go on this fabulous trip which I knew they would thoroughly enjoy. At the same time I needed time to think about it because as their main carer I worried about them going that far away from me.

They would travel to Rovaniemi in Lapland which was a three and a half hour journey each way. So it wasn't like I could hop on a plane if they needed me. It did make a difference to me that Ger was going on the trip. We had known her since Emma and Luke were babies and I trusted her. After thinking through all the information I decided to let them go on the trip, I could not deny them the experience of going to Lapland to see Santa. I had a lump in my throat that morning as I waved goodbye to them as they set off for the Airport on the bus which collected the group from the hospital. The day was captured on a video and it was great to see some of the fun they had experienced.

Some photographs of that trip are still displayed on the walls of the hospital.

As they headed off that morning on the bus to the Airport, I saw the moon in the sky but little did we know that many years later Emma would be taking a very significant plane journey by moonlight which would either offer her a second chance at life or would dash her hopes.

We were having some fun seizing the moment to have a photo taken of the three of us. The camera is hanging on the clothes line and is on self-timer. One of the comments that is made the most is that Emma and Luke both look so well. This is true but to give the balance we are dealing with an illness that affects the person internally.

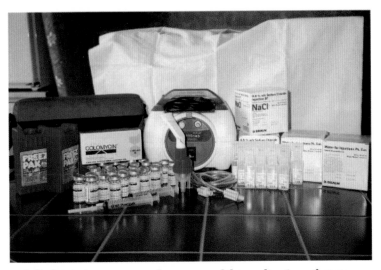

I think it is important to show some of the medications that were keeping them well. This would have been some of their nebulised medication for a week. I don't have a photo of their oral medications for this time.

4

IVs Introduced to the Regime

If I were to search for the positives of living with long term illness, one of them would be that it has taught me some important lessons about life. Life is short and one of the things I have learnt over the years is to live the moment. If the moment was good, I would enjoy it. If the moment was challenging or awful, I would try to remind myself that this could not last forever, the moment would pass and things would be manageable again. My relationship with God has kept me centered. It's such a relief to be able to talk to God in prayer and share everything with Him. I believed He was always with us. In the bad times I could share with Him all my worries and concerns and He gave me such peace that He was holding us, providing for us and protecting us through the hardships we were facing.

When Emma was seven she had her first stay in hospital. I had taken her there because I was concerned about her health. On doing some regular tests they found she had a chronic chest infection which needed a course of IV antibiotics to help bring the infection under control. So it was recommended that Emma be admitted to hospital. My parents moved into our home to look after Luke. I was going back and forward to the hospital every day to be with Emma. The first night was difficult leaving her at the hospital. She looked so small in the hospital bed and I wondered how she would cope with staying there overnight. I wanted to stay there with her but I knew I also needed to spend time with Luke. However when I arrived at the hospital ward the next morning, she was in great form. She had stayed up late talking with one or two of the teenagers. One of the girls was particularly encouraging to Emma during her hospital stay. This teenage girl had been in hospital lots of times to have treatment for her CF and she knew the hospital routine. Years later I met this girl's brother in a different hospital, he also had CF. I was delighted when I realized who he was and I enthusiastically asked him how she was doing. We had such special memories of her as she had been so kind to Emma on her first hospital stay but we had not seen her since that time. He quietly answered me so Emma would not hear while he told me that his sister had died. Tears instantly came to my eyes and a lump to my throat on hearing this. I kept thinking how brave he was. His sister had died of the same illness that he had, so he not only had to cope with her death but also the knowledge that this was ahead for him too at some stage. CF is such an awful illness and the young people who have it are so brave the way they face the day to day realities of living with long term illness.

During Emma's first hospital stay she responded well to the antibiotics and the infection cleared to a manageable level. She was used to me being her main carer and when the nurses would give her the morning dose of medication, she would wait till I came to the hospital in the morning and had checked her medicines before she would take them. I divided my time between being with Emma at the hospital and spending time with Luke. Emma's cannula, through which she would be given her IV's, was in a vein in the crease of her elbow. They put a small board on the other side of her elbow to keep her arm straight which would minimise the risk of the cannula being dislodged. With her arm out straight, she needed help with dressing and eating and anything that required her to use her left arm. It did make things more difficult but the cannula stayed in place for the 14 days so she did not need a cannula resited in another vein.

I had heard that some of the parents had learnt to do the IV antibiotics at home and so I asked Ger if I could be trained for home IV's. I knew it would be stressful for me to administer the IV's as I had no formal nursing training but at the same time it would reduce the exhaustion of traveling back and forwards to the hospital by bus and car. So the following year when Emma was eight years old and a chest x-ray showed up another infection, it was agreed that while she was in hospital, Ger would train me in how to administer the IV antibiotics.

Treatment has changed over the years but in those days the home IV system was a bit more complicated than it is now. We used a Sidekick system. It was a compact system using a small pump about the size of the palm of my hand and because it was portable Emma was able to walk around while the IV antibiotics were going into her veins. The medicine is prepared and then mixed with sterile water and put into the bag. This is then put into the middle of the Sidekick pump and when the lid is closed, the pressure on the bag pushes out the medicine through the tube into the patient over the required period of time, usually 30 or 40 minutes. There was a flush of sodium chloride to be given before and after. Another antibiotic was also administered over a shorter period of time in a different way. Ger was great at training me to administer IV's, I have always appreciated her efficiency and her dedication to her job and patients. She would explain things clearly and then give me space to prepare the medicine without standing over my shoulder making me nervous. I was so stressed out with all that we were going through preparing for Christmas, dividing my time between being at the hospital with Emma and spending time at home with Luke. Mum and Dad had moved into our home again to help look after him. Of course the biggest stress was learning a new skill that came with huge responsibilities.

The moment came when my training was complete and I was to administer my first dose of IV antibiotics to Emma. She was sitting comfortably on a chair in Ger's office. I carefully and nervously followed the procedure I had been trained to do. Thankfully I didn't have to inject into her skin as there is a small piece at the end of her cannula line that I would administer the medication through. As I began giving the IV antibiotics, Emma shouted out in a panicky voice that she could not feel her legs. I clamped off the line immediately so the medicine would stop going through to Emma's veins and I told Ger there was a problem with Emma's legs.. Ger reassured me that it was probably just because she had been sitting for a while that her legs felt a bit odd. She said Emma would be fine when she could walk around for a few minutes and encouraged me to continue giving the IV's. Sure enough when Emma started walking around again, her legs were fine. Over the years since then we have often thought of the funny side of the situation that day although it was far from amusing at the time.

On that hospital stay I administered 3 days of Emma's IV treatment under Ger's instruction. Ventolin by nebuliser was given to Emma to help her breathe properly and as she had developed another complication of CF, steroids were added to her daily treatment to help relieve the symptoms of wheeziness.

I remember on this hospital admission we met the family of a young teenage boy who had CF. He was coughing up huge amounts of a murky coloured mucus and that day he was going to see the consultant to tell him what his decision was about whether or not to have a heart and lung transplant. I remember thinking how brave he was, in his early teen years to be making such a huge decision. His mother said to me that it would be his decision and they would stand by him whatever he decided. The young lad made the decision to have the heart and lung transplant and by the time we met the family again, years later, he had been through the operation and was doing very well.

Four months later when Emma came off her steroid treatment the wheeziness returned and a return visit to the hospital with a subsequent x-ray showed that the infection was back in her lung in the exact place it had been before. Another IV course was needed to clear this infection. As I had been trained to do the IV's by now, Emma only had to stay in hospital for 3 days and then I was allowed to complete the rest of the course at home.

As part of my training I had been told what side effects to look out for and if any of these presented themselves I was to phone the hospital immediately. In the early days of me doing home IV's, the medicines had to be collected at a central pharmacy in the Pheonix Park on the far side of the city to where we were living. The pharmacy was open for about five hours each day. I would phone beforehand to make sure the order was ready for collection before I trekked across the city to collect them. At home I had always tried to keep their medicines out of sight so they were not constantly reminded of them. However, at times of home IV's I could not do this because we have a small house and there was no spare cupboard space.

There were many good reasons for choosing to do home IV's. The children were in their home environment which I always believed encouraged them to feel better. They could sleep in their own bed and have familiar things around them. They could rest when they wanted to and they were eating all the foods they were used to. They could even continue to go to school, with the exception of the days when they had hospital visits, so they did not fall behind in their lessons. They just had to be careful not to dislodge the cannula in their hand. Doing home IV's meant I was also able to continue to do the child minding jobs I had taken on to help with paying the bills.

For the two weeks of the IV's, Emma was restricted in her activities as she had to be careful the cannula did not fall out. So before or after the IV course I always made the effort to have a special treat for them, like going bowling or having a meal out somewhere. I felt it was important for them to have some fun before having to cope with the restrictions of the two weeks of the treatment.

I did find the early days of doing home IV's very stressful and exhausting because the routine was very demanding. I am a night owl but don't deal too well with early mornings or lack of sleep. So the routine of a 5.30am start, to be ready for the 6pm dose, but also having a late night at 11.30pm, by the time the 10pm dose was finished, was very tiring.

The two IV antibiotics would take about an hour to go through. Emma could sleep through the early morning and late night doses which was good as she needed all the sleep she could get to help fight the infections. The 2pm dose in the middle of the day was manageable because I was already up and about in my daily routine. I would collect the children early from school so we were home in time for this dose. In those early days I had to have total quiet to concentrate on all the preparations of the medicine to make sure everything was done correctly. As time went on I became more relaxed about doing home IV's I could talk to people while I was preparing the medicine because it had become second nature to me by then.

I never slept much the first night because even though I had set the alarm clock I was afraid I would sleep through and miss the first dose of antibiotics. After the first 24 hours the exhaustion was kicking in, as I was only getting about 6 hours sleep a night, so I had no problem falling asleep when I eventually got to bed. The nights that were particularly difficult were the ones where I would get to bed around midnight but then Emma would need physiotherapy anytime between 1am and 3am in the morning. By the time I had finished doing the physiotherapy I was so awake it would be hard to fall asleep again.

There were other times when Emma's vein would reject the cannula and we would go immediately to the hospital, regardless of the time of night or day, to have a cannula resited in another vein so that we didn't miss out on a dose.

At the end of the course I would remove the cannula from the vein. The first time was nerve racking, swabbing the bandages with the Remove wipe to make it easier to peel off the layers of bandages and then slowly taking the needle out of her vein. I felt a bit sick but the next time was not as daunting.

At the end of this course of home IV's, the Consultant decided that Emma should have regular IV's every six months.

I learnt during the tough times to take one day at a time. When things were unbearably tough I would focus on taking a minute at a time.

Always, I prayed lots.

Everyone has a different experience of CF depending on the level of CF that they have.

Through all this time when Emma's health was not good, Luke was keeping reasonably well. He had all the usual daily treatment of physiotherapy, oral medicines and nebulisers. He had the regular clinic check ups, an Annual Assessment, the yearly Flu Vaccine and regular changes to his medication routine to keep him in the best health.

Luke didn't need his first course of IV antibiotics until he was eight years old. At a routine clinic visit they discovered his lung function was down 30%. They were also concerned that he had not put on a lot of weight in the previous six months. Both of these can be a sign of infection. He had already had a course of oral antibiotics but was still chesty and unwell.

By now we had a new Consultant, Dr. Greally, who was looking after Emma and Luke's medical care. Luke was against the idea of IV's. He didn't want the cannula in his vein as it restricted his activities like playing football. As I was already trained to do home IV's, Luke would not have to stay in hospital. Dr. Greally asked me if I wanted to do Emma and Luke's IV's at the same time or if I wanted to do Emma's for two weeks and then Luke's for the following two weeks. My thinking on it was that I would be exhausted for the two weeks anyway so doing both at the same time would be better. If I did the IV's one fortnight after the other I would have to deal with that level of tiredness and stress for a month. We had time to think about this and to prepare Luke for the course of treatment. I gave my decision to the CF team that I would like to do both IV courses at the same time. Emma had already had IVs one month previous to this so the timing would not work for this course of IV's but would be taken into consideration for future courses.

They scheduled in a date for Luke's first IV. A cough swab had been taken and sent to the laboratory for analysis to see what infections were present and then based on the results they would select the most effective antibiotics. With this IV course two antibiotics would be administered three times a day. Unfortunately one of the antibiotics, which was effective for the infections that Luke had at the time, is known to sting the veins and he was in agony as the first dose was being given.

The first dose is always done in the hospital and if it is a new antibiotic we would have to return that evening to have the second dose in the hospital. It's a safety precaution in case the patient has a reaction to the antibiotic.

When we returned to the hospital that evening I distracted Luke, by walking up and down the corridor with him when the medicine was going through so that he would be less aware of the pain. There were only one or two murmers of pain from him compared to the agony of that afternoon. As this particular antibiotic is rough on the veins, they are likely to collapse more often.

Day three, we had to return for levels. This is a blood test done before and after the first antibiotic is given. It is important to have these pre and post levels done to check what level of antibiotic is in the person's system. If the antibiotic level is too low it will not clear the infection. If the antibiotic level is too high there can be negative side effects.

Luke had his pre levels done but when I was giving him the afternoon dose of antibiotics the cannula would not work so he needed a new one.

The next day Ger phoned with the results of his levels. They were slightly low so she told me the new dosage to give him which took into account the extra amount of antibiotic he needed. An appointment was also made for us to return to the hospital the following Monday where they would repeat his levels. A lung function test would also be done and a cough swab taken. These would be sent to the laboratory to check how much of the infection had cleared during the IV course.

Day five...he played some football. Prepare for cannula resite.

Day six...cannula resite needed. Return to hospital to have the new cannula inserted. It was very painful for him as it took three attempts to get a suitable vein.

The rest of the course was manageable in the sense that the extra demands on us at that time were running smoothly. We had learnt to live with crisis and difficulties as part of our everyday lives. I noticed over the years that sometimes when I told people, in answer to their questions, how things were with us, they would think we were going through a terrible time. We were, it's just that our tolerance of awfulness was increasing because we had so much to cope with. It's like having a high pain threshold, except ours was a high threshold of coping with awful circumstances. Often our reactions to things that would send others into a tailspin were different because we had become accustomed to living with crisis.

On this occasion we had returned to the hospital for a review to see if the IV course had cleared the infection but sometimes Ger would come out to our house to do a home visit near the end of an IV course and this would save us the trip to the hospital.

In the phlebotomy department, one of the nurses used to call us the 'Triplets' because if one went in for a blood test we all went into the room together. That was the only way I knew how to do things, if one of them was going through something I wanted to be there with them to support them through it. I believe that one of the positives of long term illness is that it drew us closer as a family unit as we spent more time together because of their health care regime.

This is what Emma remembers about her experience of home IV's...

When Mum explained to me that she was going to be trained to do home IV's I wasn't keen on the idea at first. I had been used to the nurses doing this. The nurses gave IV's as part of their jobs everyday. It wasn't that I didn't trust Mum but they were experts and I was comfortable with that situation. The day Mum began her training I remember the little room Mum was trained in. I was sitting on a chair, with my cannula already in,waiting for Mum to give me my first dose. She came over to me and started injecting the dose into my cannula. I (being a bit of a drama queen) screamed " I can't feel my legs. I can't feel my legs" As it was her first time, Mum stopped giving the medicine, immediately thinking the worst. She thought she had paralyzed me but Ger explained that it wasn't possible to do so with IV's,. She assured Mum that I was ok and to continue giving me the treatment. Ger said that my legs had probably gone dead because I was sitting down for so long. When Mum had finished linking me up to my first antibiotic I went for a walk and my legs were fine.

I'm glad Mum decided to learn how to do the IV's at home. When I had to stay in hospital to have my treatment I was bored out of my mind. It really makes you appreciate home. When Mum started IV's at home I was still restricted in what I could do because cannula's are fragile but at least I could go to school with my friends and be in my own surroundings at home.

When I had to go on IV's it meant being restricted for the next two weeks. I couldn't even do simple things like tie my shoe laces or cut my dinner so I was depending on Mum a lot. A few days into the treatment and I was screaming to do anything...even household chores. Now that's bad! At break times in school , I had to stay indoors so that my cannula would not get knocked out of place. If it did, I would need a cannula resite.

It was such an inconvenience that I didn't want at that age. I was young I should have been playing outside like my friends but playing outside was not a thing I was going to risk for a resite (friends did come and sit or play with me at school in the first aid room though). Cannulas are really sore to get in place and I never had (and still don't have) good veins. My veins are thin, small, very hard to find and not a lot are big enough to use so I guarded my cannula's with my life. It took a long time for anyone to find a vein so I was going to do anything and everything it took to keep the canula in.

Despite the fact I had to stay in at break times, school was great. I loved it. It was one of the very few things I could do while on IV's and I saw my friends for a while. Whereas if I was in hospital I would be watching television and staring at the same four walls all day.

I also had to go home early from school which I didn't like because going home meant it was time for an hour of medicine through my veins, a cannula resite if the cannula would not work and also not having much to do for the afternoon because of the restrictions of the cannula. At those times I was losing out on seeing my friends for a few more minutes than I could have seen them in school because I had to have my meds. I was actually happy if my cannula was in my left hand because I could do my homework, that's how desperate I was to do something. The thing was that I felt well on the IV's so sitting down doing nothing was hard. I'm also one of those people that prefers to be doing something a lot of the time so that made it even harder.

This is what Luke remembers about his experience of home IV's...

I always remember detesting IV's. However, it was a plus to have them at home where I was in my normal surrounding and had everything I needed. I never had to have IV's in hospital because Mum had already learnt how to do them at home for Emma. Most of the time you could feel the medicine going through your veins with a cannula. It was mainly cold but there was one medicine that was known for stinging your veins. It hurt so much but my Mum read football stories to me to get my mind off the pain. That always worked for me.

IV's changed all of our sleeping patterns and I woke up sometimes when Mum came into my bedroom to do them. That was 10 at night ,6 in the morning. I got off school early cause we had an afternoon dose of IV's at 2pm. My friends in school were very supportive when I had IV's. They helped me when I needed it and they took turns to stay in at breaktime with me and keep me company. I thought everyone knew what the IV's were for but there was one day in the second year of me having IV's when one person in my class asked questions about it. Other people in my class told her instead of me as they all knew. Years later, I even had a teacher who wrote on my school report that I did well in his class except for when my arm was broken. But I was in secondary school by then and because I did not like people knowing I had a cannula in my arm he had mistaken the bandage over my cannula for a cast which he thought was for a broken arm.

I did not like having IV's mainly because I wasn't able to play sports for two weeks and I love sports. I went through 6 canulas in 10 days on one course of IV's but

*one of those resites was because I played football with the
cannula in.*

5

It Should Have Been Fun

As I mentioned earlier, CF is one illness where the treatment is constantly improving and helping the sufferer to live a longer life.

When Emma was eleven years old she began a new medication. It was an antibiotic which would be used to help manage the CF bacteria present on her lungs. It was given by nebuliser twice daily and would take about 15 mins for it to be administered. It was alternated with her usual morning and evening nebuliser. So for twenty-eight days she would be on the new nebulised medication and then she would switch back to the usual medication for the next twenty-eight days. After that she would revert back to the new one and so the cycle continued.

Dr. Greally had mentioned that he would like to start Emma on this medication and an appointment was made for her to go to hospital for the first dose. I would always talk through things with Emma and Luke to prepare them for what was ahead so I discussed this with Emma to let her know it was something that was being added to her treatment to help keep her well.

When the day arrived for her to start this treatment we went to the hospital and some routine checks were done before she was to be given the first dose.

One of the tests to be done was an oxygen saturation test which measures the amount of oxygen being carried in the blood. The test is quick and painless. A small sensor is placed on one of her fingers and the reading comes up on the screen of the machine within minutes. When her oxygen saturation test showed a reading below acceptable levels we knew the possible cause of this low reading.

Emma is very creative and has always enjoyed art, drawing and making cards. She often did projects like rubber stamping designs on cards the size of gift tags and colouring the designs to perfection. The gift tags were beautiful and anyone who got one on a present kept it as it was too good to throw away.

Months prior to this hospital visit we had heard about an art camp and after finding out more about this we signed her up for a two week camp. She would be spending the morning and afternoon there so we would be able to fit her nebulisers, medicine and physiotherapy around the camp times.

A neighbour's child was going to camp as well and this meant we were able to share the lifts there and back. Emma was so excited about all the crafts she would do and learn there. The first week went well but I noticed near the end of that week that her breathing was not good. She was unusually wheezy. I talked with her and discovered that on on the lunch time walks they had to beat back the bushes to find the path. They also sat on haystacks to have their lunch. The pollen involved in both of these activities were having an adverse effect on Emma's breathing.

Early into the second week, her breathing was so tight that I had to take her out of camp early for the sake of her health. She had looked forward to this for so long and I was heartbroken for her that she could not complete the two weeks of camp.

As her mother, I was also upset for her when I heard about how she was struggling to keep up with the other children who could walk or run up the hill to the art cabins, yet she was lagging behind because she couldn't breathe. I could feel her loneliness of seeing the others race ahead and no-one walking with her. I wished I was there with her so I could carry her up the hill or even just walk beside her so she was not alone. CF is such a heartbreaking disease. She was only eleven and already she was having to deal with the disappointments and limitations of her health.

To help improve her breathing, I increased her daily physiotherapy and gave her Ventolin when she needed it.

The day we went to the hospital for the first dose of the new nebulised medicine, they gave it to her but she was also given a two week course of oral antibiotics and steroids for the wheeziness. By the end of this course of antibiotics her health had not improved much and she needed a further week of antibiotics. She was reviewed a week after this and her lung function was still down considerably. An immediate course of IV antibiotics was needed. As this was an unexpected course, she would have to go into hospital for the first few days and then I would be allowed to take her home to complete the treatment.

One of the things I noticed with Emma was that when she got bad news about her health, she would have her moments of crying or being annoyed but then she would get on with whatever course of action needed to be taken. I think when people have a difficult path in life they are given extra qualities, like bravery and maturity, that help them cope with the difficulties they have to face.

Another thing that living with a long term illness taught me is that life can be unpredictable. At a moment's notice, we could be plunged into a crisis with either Emma or Luke's health. We had to be prepared for anything. With long term illness there are good days and bad days but there are no days off.

Emma was in hospital this time for four days so they could monitor her oxygen levels and make some changes to her medication. On hearing that she was in hospital, family and friends came to visit her. Luke was still very young and every day I brought him to the hospital with me so we could spend as much time as possible with Emma. Again I coped by dealing with the priorities each day. It was exhausting going back and forwards to the hospital. Dr. Greally reluctantly let her home after four days and I completed the course of IV treatment.

By now there was a welcome, stress-reducing change in the home IV system as regards the supplies, they were now delivered directly to our home. We just had to arrange with the company delivering them that we would be home to take in the delivery or arrange to have a neighbour take them in if we were at the hospital.

Also, one of the medicines now came fully prepared in a type of bottle. It was a compact, portable system which was the size of the palm of my hand. There is a bubble inside it which is filled with the antibiotic. When the attached line is primed and then connected to the patient's line, the medicine flows through at a set rate until all the medicine has gone into the patient. One of the benefits of this system is that it saves time compared to the Sidekick system we had been using.

By the end of the course of IV treatment, Emma's lung function had only increased a small amount. Dr Greally discussed with us the possibility of her going on 4 monthly IV's rather than 6 monthly IV's. I prayed and hoped this would not happen.

One of the things I have always appreciated about   Dr Greally is that he really listens to what I say and will take this into consideration. On this occasion I asked him if we could have more time to see if things improved. She still had some extra treatments to get through before Christmas. Thankfully he agreed and an appointment was set for the New Year to discuss this further. He also introduced the idea of having a port inserted if she needed to go on 4 monthly IV's.

Cannula's can be unpredictable in that we never knew how long they were going to last. Sometimes the vein rejects the cannula or sometimes the cannula slips out of the vein. Emma had a cannula that lasted the full 14 days of an IV course but Luke had 6 cannula resites during a 10 day IV course. The positives of having a port inserted is that it is attached permanently to a deeper vein in the arm or the chest. At the beginning of an IV course the port would be needled and the needle would stay in place for the whole IV course. It is less troublesome than a cannula. Emma rejected both of these ideas for now - the more regular IV's and the port, but soon she would have to consider them again. Thankfully at the next clinic visit it was decided that she could stay on the 6 monthly IV's for the moment.

6

Enough is Enough

When Luke was 12 and Emma was 13 years old, I had been doing home IV's twice yearly for 4 years with scheduled IV's in the Summer and nearer Christmas. At some point in the course of IV's the vein would reject the cannula and a painful resites would follow as it was sometimes difficult to find a suitable vein. If a resite was needed at the 11pm dose, I would bring them back to hospital straight away for a new cannula to be put in place even though it meant we would not get home until the early hours of the morning, I felt it was important to get the resite done as if we waited until the following morning that would have been two doses missed, 11pm and 7am.

As Luke needed 6 resites in ten days on one IV course, the matter of the port needed to be considered again. The port or portacather would be inserted into his arm and attached to a deeper vein. It would always stay in place and would be flushed out every 28 days to keep it clear and working. I would have the option of learning how to flush the port at home to save us going to the hospital every month to have it done. I wasn't at the point of feeling comfortable putting a needle into their skin to do the flush so I chose to return to the hospital for the monthly port flushes. The port can last any length of time from 6 months to 10 years but the average lifespan is 5 years. It saves all the hassle of having a cannula in as the centre of it just needs to be needled at the beginning of a course of treatment. There is none of the hassle of trying to find a suitable vein. After their port was inserted I would be retrained for home IV's as giving antibiotics intravenously via a port would be a sterile procedure. I would have to learn all about positive pressure and non-touch techniques.

Over time I had a lot of discussions with Emma about the port. One of these discussions was at midnight. They were both on home IV's at the time. I had finished the night time dose of IV antibiotics for both of them and was passing by Emma's bedroom. I noticed that she was sitting up in her bed in the dark. I asked her what was wrong and all her questions going through her mind about the port came tumbling out. She was a young teenager by now and had always thought through things thoroughly before reaching a decision. For the next half an hour we discussed things like the necessity of IV's, the unfairness of CF, the operation to insert the port and her worries about the operation. She was even worried that if they found a cure for CF, our Nurse Specialist Ger would not have a job anymore. I think talking about these things helped her and it also helped that Luke was very much in favour of getting his port. His acceptance of it encouraged Emma to have a port inserted.

So it was scheduled for their next course of treatment which would be at the beginning of December. For a good few years it seemed that we always had a major health crisis coming up to Christmas.

Before the port was inserted Emma and Luke would have a week of home IV's to have their lungs in the best possible condition for this. Then they would be admitted to hospital to have the port operation under general anestethic. The home IV's went as usual. A vein was found for the cannula on the second attempt for both of them. They were both on different antibiotics as they had different infections that needed to be treated. I continued the treatment at home with daily doses at 7am 3pm and 11pm. It meant the usual early start at 6.30pm and not getting to bed until after midnight. Over the next five days we were back and forward to the hospital three times for levels, repeat levels and a cannula resite. Also the hospital had phoned to say the result of a test showed Luke's levels were too high and they told me the new quantity of medication to give to him instead. The next day Emma and Luke were admitted to hospital for the port operation. This was Luke's first time to stay in hospital because of his CF as I had always done his treatment at home. I stayed over in the hospital that night in parent's accommodation. Ger suggested that I might try to get as much rest as possible as the next day would be emotionally demanding.

Emma was the first one to have the pre med to relax her before the operation. She has always been very flexible and can easily cross her legs in the lotus position. So when she did this and leaned forward with her head resting on her legs, I thought she was just getting comfortable, until I heard her say 'Help'. She was so relaxed that she couldn't get back up. Luke thought this was hilarious and had great fun listening to the funny things she was saying under the influence of the pre med. When the time came I went down to theatre with Emma and a nurse. I was allowed to go into the pre theatre room with her and stay until she had the anaesthetic.

Although I didn't have someone physically present with me, I felt comforted that friends and family were praying for us and in touch by text messages. My faith in God carried me through as well because I believed God was with us every step of the way.

When I went back to the ward, Luke was due to have his pre med soon. It had a different effect on him and he went very quiet. Shortly I was told that Emma was in recovery and I could go down with Luke to the waiting area. I remember being in the waiting area with Luke and hearing the physiotherapist talking to Emma in the recovery room. I was waiting for Luke to be called into the pre theatre room for his anestethic but Emma wanted to see me as she was coming round from her operation. I said to Luke that I would just go and talk to Emma and then come back to him. He would still be able to see me from where he was sitting in the wheelchair. I went to Emma and choking back the tears I told her how brave she had been and that she was a great girl. The physiotherapist, Diane, was so encouraging, had a great sense of humour and was a very cheerful person to deal with. In a very short while they were taking Emma back to the ward so I went back to Luke.

He was upset but couldn't say why. Thankfully the theatre team didn't take too long and when they called Luke into the pre-theatre room, we went through the same process as I had with Emma …ten…nine…eight…he was out cold and I left the room crying again. It always upset me to see them out cold. I had my cry and then I went up to the ward to be with Emma as she was coming round from her anaesthetic. They would come to find me on the ward when Luke was out of theatre. They say that whatever way you go into the anaesthetic is the way you come out of it. Sure enough when I went down to the recovery room later when Luke was through the operation, he was very emotional. He could not focus his vision very well and this was upsetting him. He calmed shortly and we went up to the ward.

They both recovered well for the rest of the day. I slept in parent's accommodation at the hospital that night as both Emma and Luke were to stay in hospital for a few more days.

I was woken in the early hours of the morning by someone knocking on my door. One of the nurses asked me to come to the ward as Emma was upset and needed me. She had come out in a rash and was imagining all sorts of things it could be. It was possibly a reaction to something in theatre earlier that day. Anyway one of the doctors was able to give her something to take the rash away. I was going to sleep in the chair beside her bed but, when the rash had gone down, the doctor suggested I would be more comfortable in the parent's accommodation. They would call me again if Emma or Luke needed me.

The port was not used for the first twenty-four hours and then after that it was flushed to see that it was working properly. Emma and Luke were to stay in hospital for a few more days to complete the course of IV antibiotics.

The ward Emma and Luke were in went quiet at the weekend, they were the only two patients in it. This gave them the opportunity to plug their dance mat into the television and that's when the fun started. As they would try to get anyone who came into the ward to try dancing on it. Emma was in great form as she was feeling well coming near the end of the course of IV's. Also her fears about the port operation were in the past now. Luke, on the other hand, was deteriorating with each day. It started with him not being able to tolerate food and progressed to him not being able to tolerate his oral medicines or water.

It was discovered that he had had a reaction to one of the antibiotics he was on and now his levels were going higher by the day.

He was taken off the antibiotic and then had regular blood tests three times daily to monitor his levels to make sure they were coming down to an acceptable level. Dr Greally kept in regular contact with me to give us results of blood tests as soon as they became available. The CF team were also there to answer any questions we had.

Thankfully his levels came down to an acceptable level, over the next while. As we had discovered at other times of crisis, life goes on. All of us only have a certain amount of energy for each day so I channeled my energy into being there for Luke and helping us all through the situation.

Emma was out of hospital by now so in the mornings I would leave her to school and then go to the hospital to be with Luke. I was child minding at the time to help pay the bills so I brought the baby to the hospital to mind him there. I was blessed to have the help of my parents and friends who would help out with Emma's routine when they could.

I had always said it would be time enough for Luke to have a mobile when he went to secondary school but now I felt it was essential for him to have this as it was his first time in hospital. He would be happier if he could contact me whenever he needed to.

Coping with Luke's health crisis and basic survival at a time like this was enough. Although when you have two unwell children in the family, there are always unexpected extras that crop up from time to time. One of these unexpected times was when Luke's health was improving but he was still in hospital.

There was a concert there one night and he was allowed to go to it. Mum and Dad minded Emma at our home so I could stay with Luke. When I came home from the hospital later that night, exhausted, Emma needed a bandage changed on her port site. I switched on her bedroom light so I could see to change her bandage but unfortunately this woke her and she got a coughing fit.

She was tired and didn't want to co-operate with physiotherapy and deep breaths. This was followed with her throwing up mucus all over the bathroom sink and floor. My body ached as I cleaned it all up before falling into bed exhausted.

My prayers, again, were for strength to get through each day.

Each year at Christmas we visited Ronan, my counsellor friend, who lived near to the hospital. This year was no different, the hospital allowed Luke out for three hours so he could be included in our annual trip. I knew if we needed to get Luke back to the hospital quickly we were near enough. It was always tough bringing either Emma or Luke back to the hospital after having them home or out of the hospital for a few hours. To have to settle them in hospital again and then go home without them was difficult.

A few days before Christmas Luke was allowed to come home. He was so happy, he kept talking and laughing. He had missed almost the whole month of December in school and wanted very much to see his friends before the Christmas holidays. We went straight from the hospital to the school Carol Service. It was great to see everyone and to get such a warm welcome. It was lovely to sit and enjoy some normality again.

This is what Emma remembers about having a port….

The way I ended up getting the port in is very funny. I was very reluctant to get one. Every time I was asked, I said no. I got tired of the discussions about the port so in the end I said " Ok, if Luke gets the port I will" Thinking he wouldn't. Surprisingly, right there and then without hesitation Luke says "Ok, I'll get it". Mum, Ger (the CF nurse) and Luke just laughed. Anyway that's how I ended up getting it. It made it easier that Luke and I were getting it at the same day one after another.

The day of the operation came. I was worried but I went ahead with it. Before I went in I was told that my arm would be hard and sore to move for a few days but I would still have to do exercises with my arm because it would help it to heal. So being the person I am, thinking the worst, I was expecting my arm to be throbbing. It was nothing of the sort. When I woke up, I was wondering what all the fuss was about. It wasn't as sore as it could be and I could move my arm pretty well. I could just touch my shoulder which they said was really good. They didn't expect I'd be able to do that so quickly.

That night I woke up with a very itchy stomach. When I looked at it, I saw a rash. It was the early hours of the morning and I was tired. I started to cry (but not that loud). Luke woke up and asked if I was ok. I snapped at him " I'm fine".

A nurse called Dean Martin (I'm serious, that's his real name), obviously heard me crying and came down to the ward to see if I was ok. I wouldn't tell him. The next thing I remember is Mum sitting by my bed till I fell back asleep.

I stayed in hospital for a few more days and then I was allowed home.

We had great fun those days because the ward wasn't very busy. We even had the nurses on the dance mat that we got as a present.

I never regretted getting the port in. I, at that stage, needed IV's every 6 months so it was very handy. All they had to do was find the middle of the port and put the needle in. That would last for the whole course of IV's which meant no canulas and no resites. I also had a bit more freedom. It was much better than being poked and proded every time I needed a cannula for my IV's.

This is what Luke remembers about having a port...

As you have probably read I haven't had the best luck with the cannulas. I just couldn't sit still for two weeks without playing football so when I heard that I could get a port inserted and wouldn't need anymore resites, I was very interested.

The way that Emma and I came to the decision was that she said "I'll get it if Luke will". She thought that I wouldn't say yes and she was surprised when I said ok. I was nervous as you would be going into an operation but I was in safe hands.

Emma and I had to have an IV course for a week before the operation so that we were in the best of health. The day of the operation we were admitted to the Beech ward. Emma was to go first. She was given her pre-medicine that would relax her before the anesthetic. It was great, she began to be drowsy and just made me laugh for ages with the things she was saying and doing. It was hilarious. Then it was my turn. I got the pre-medicine and they said that I should stay seated as you become very drowsy after a few seconds. I didn't believe them and stood up after I took it and said it isn't working. I was told to sit down and then two seconds later I was out like a light (well so I thought).

The next thing I remember I going in a wheelchair past the recovery room and saw Emma. I don't know why but I just began to cry. Then next I went into the operating theatre where I got the anesthetic and I started to have a very sharp pain up my arm. It was just the anesthetic going through my body. I was out for few hours. When I woke up I thought that I was blind and I could only see in black and white. I was very scared but then just fell asleep. I woke up and was told to roll over onto another bed but then I looked at my arms that had two cannulas and a port. I refused to roll over just in case I knocked one of them out. I eventually went onto the other bed and fell asleep again. It took a while for the anesthetic to wear off. Emma and I had to spend a week more in the hospital just to finish the course but when it came to that day, Emma was discharged but I wasn't. I had a reaction to one of the medicines and couldn't eat or even drink water. Some of my levels went a lot higher than they should have. They peaked and came down over the next while. My mum would come in everyday to be at the hospital with me and sometimes had the baby she was minding with her. The nurses in the hospital were very good to me and made the stay in hospital more fun. I was discharged a day or two before Christmas. All in all I never regretted getting a port in. It has saved me getting loads of cannula resites. I feel more confident to do things while the port is in than when a cannula was in. It was handier to get the port needled rather that being poked every time I needed a cannula resite.

7

Time for Fun

It wasn't all doom and gloom. We have many memories of happy times as the children were growing up. I think having to cope with so much awfulness gave me a greater appreciation of the better moments when we were not in the middle of a crisis. We would seize those times and bask in the normality of when things were calm.

Holiday times were few and far between as we did not have spare cash to afford one and also I did not want to be too far away from our usual hospital in case there was an unexpected health crisis. When times of respite did arrive they were much needed and greatly appreciated. One of these times was when Emma and Luke were offered a place in Barretstown for a holiday.

Barretstown is in Co. Wicklow. It was started by the actor Paul Newman and is based on the American style of camps that are funded by him. Children, from Ireland and European countries, who have a long term illness qualify for a short stay there to help give their families a much need rest. While the children are there, they are given their medicine by qualified staff but the focus of their time there is on fun, enjoying themselves and trying out new activities. It helps the children gain confidence and boosts their self esteem.

Emma, Luke and I worked together as a team in living with their CF so at the first mention of them going away for this holiday, the issue of separation anxiety was present in all of us. I couldn't deny them the chance of this holiday but as I was the one who was their main carer, I worried about handing over the day to day care to someone else. I worried right up till the time I drove in the gates of Barretstown and then all that worry disappeared.

The driveway was lined with trees, there were horses in the fields and at the end of it there was plenty of green open space, a lake for fishing, a beautiful old castle and a welcoming party. We were a bit early but as I parked the car the volunteers came over to greet us. We didn't even have to introduce ourselves, when they heard that both of the children were staying they said "Well then this must be Emma and Luke". I choked back the tears at the warmth of the welcome. I knew Emma and Luke would be well looked after and would have a good time.

One or two of the volunteers brought Emma and Luke's luggage to their chalets and the rest of the volunteers brought us to the chalet where the medicine would be done. The medical team went through the list of medication and arranged times in the day when Emma and Luke would know to come over for their medicine and nebulisers. It was such a relief to know everything was so well organized.

After that we went through the courtyard, past the art room and on towards the chalets. Inside the chalets was fabulous. There was a main room with couches and easy chairs. The bedrooms had pine beds with blanket boxes at the end of them. They would be sharing the chalets with children from different nationalities and also children who had different illnesses. I said my goodbyes quickly because I didn't want to upset us all by crying in front of them. As I drove away down the tree lined driveway I was glad I had brought my Dad with me for company. I talked endlessly to stop myself from crying. I had organized different things for that week so that I wasn't sitting around wishing the hours away until they were home again. I arranged a massage and body wrap so that I could be pampered and have plenty of relaxation. I went out to dinner once or twice with friends also.

They both had a fabulous time and when I went to collect them they told me about all the activities like fishing, climbing, archery, drama, arts and crafts. The night before they came home there was a dance. They were collected in beautiful old style cars and driven out of the grounds into the village. When they came back, a red carpet lined the way into the dance. When I heard about this, I thought it was lovely for the staff there to add all these extras to make the evening special for the children.

This is what Luke remembers about his holiday in Barretstown....

I thought that Barretstown was an amazing experience. All the staff were really nice to me. I was staying in a cottage with Finnish, English and Irish children. We did many activities like archery and canoeing. On the last night they brought us out of the grounds and back to the main hall in old fashioned cars for our final night activity which was a disco. They even went out of their way and put out a red carpet that made us feel like celebrities. The staff were amazing and it was great fun making new friends from different countries that had gone through similar things because of living with illness.

This is what Emma remembers about Barretstown...

I had the time of my life. I'm glad I went. At first, when I was offered to go, I was unsure whether I wanted to or not. I know I wouldn't get this chance again for a long time but I was scared. It was my first time away from home, without Mum, due to the fact I hadn't been ready to take on the responsibility of my meds full time with no back up of someone who knew my routine. Eventually, I decided to go. It was a great experience. Each day was filled with activities, different, exciting activities, ones I wouldn't have ever experienced or think of trying if I hadn't gone. It was one week of early mornings and late nights.

There were 12 beautiful cottages that reminded me of the cottages in Snow White and the Seven Dwarfs. A little pathway lead up to the area where the cottage was. Off this path were little paths leading to each individual cottage. In the room where we were sleeping there were three small, low beds on each side. It was lovely. Girls and boys were in different cottages. In our cottage there were girls from England, Denmark and Ireland. All there to have a good time. All there for different reasons. All with our individual stories. Also in the cottages were 6 helpers to keep us under control.

Everyone was in different groups but we all got the opportunity to do the same things at some stage. Being in different groups was to help us meet other people but for me I was happy hanging out with the other two from my cottage. I was very shy and not very good at starting conversation. Our group was a very small one compared to others. It contained 9 kids and 5 leaders. No two days were the same. Every day was a different adventure.

It was FANTASTIC.

In the early hours in the morning, when normally you'd still be in bed, the leaders would wake you up. Everyone gathered into a big room to have beautiful breakfast. Their food was gorgeous. At every meal, when the first table finished, they started a chant made up by their cottage which contained everything; shouting, banging the table, stamping feet.

Every meal was a contest to see who's chant was the best and the loudest. It was great fun. During the day there would be four activities. Main ones were canoeing, fishing, horse riding, archery, high ropes or low ropes. Lots of creative things were done such as cottage chat. This is where your cottage sit and talk about anything. Cottage time was a time to chill out before our next activity.

There was another thing called crazy and lazy, which could be a choice between cooking or football. The helpers were really kind and great fun to hang out with. Other programmes were organized like a camp fire, talent show and surprises left in the cottages for when we came back. Not one day or minute was wasted and I've never regretted going. It was a brilliant experience that I'm glad I had the chance to have.

With the day to day care of Emma and Luke's illness I had sort of ruled out holidays by ourselves. I knew what my limitations were and I knew that I definitely did not want to be alone in a foreign country if their illness required extra attention. The thought of trying to juggle all the usual responsibilities plus dealing with a foreign hospital plus a foreign language did not sound like a holiday to me.

I felt constantly tired from the daily demands of our situation but when the children were ten and eleven and we had not had a holiday for years, I thought about a getting away for a break. I had asked Mum and Dad if they would come with us. Then the idea snowballed as my mother knew someone who offered their apartment to us for a holiday in Spain. Next I knew there were ten family members getting our passports and tickets prepared for this holiday.

Travelling with CF can be done, it just requires more organization. We had to make sure that we had medicine for the duration of the holiday and then an added week's supply just in case of an emergency. The medicine had to be kept in our hand luggage as we could not risk it being lost or damaged. If the children had the least signs of an infection before the holiday we would have to bring a back up antibiotic to have it on stand by in case the infection developed when we were away from home. We would have to take extra enzymes in case the food was particularly high in fat content.

We had to take extra precautions, such as a high factor sunblock, if the children were on medication which made them more prone to sunburn. We would need a cool pack for carrying the vials for their lunchtime nebulised medication and we would also have to check that at our destination there would be a refrigerator available to store some of the medication for the time of the holiday. For airport security checks we would need to carry a letter from Emma and Luke's consultant detailing what medicine supplies we are carrying and the necessity for carrying these. We would need to make sure they had sufficient snacks and drinks on the journey to keep up their increased calorie needs and to make sure they did not get dehydrated. For peace of mind we also needed to have the names of a local hospital or medical centre where we could go if the children had any problem with their health while away. For this particular holiday I didn't get extra insurance but if I were to go on holiday now I would make sure we were covered by extra insurance, just in case.

It's exhausting reading all this list of extra things that needed to be done and sometimes I wondered if it was worth it. After all, we were not getting a break from CF, it was coming with us. We would still have the daily regime to do, day trips would make it more awkward to fit in the lunchtime nebuliser and we would have to be up early enough in the morning to do the physiotherapy before we left.

Anyway, all things taken into account, we headed off on the adventure, trusting that God would be with us and would provide for and protect us. As it turned out everything ran smoothly. An added bonus was that the different type of heat over in Spain turned out to be much better for Emma and Luke. They were able to breathe easier. We catered for ourselves so we were able to choose foods that suited them. The holiday was just what we needed and we have many special memories from it.

8

Life Changes

I once read a quote which said 'Every experience changes us and important, intense or ecstatic experiences change us even more'. I learned the truth of this in the December of 2003.

A few months before this I had returned to work in a part-time job after being at home with the children for years. For seven of those years I had taken on child minding jobs to earn extra money to help pay the bills.

When looking for a job I realized I could only work about 20 hours a week as I was trying to combine working outside the home with also having enough time and energy for Emma and Luke's extra healthcare needs, hospital visits and regular home IV courses. I prayed I would find something suitable.

I finished my child minding jobs that June and as always I had put aside some money during the term time to buy Emma and Luke's school books when the booklist came out in June for the following September. That was one worry out of the way. July came but still no sign of a job. By August things were getting a bit desperate as the budgeted money was running tight.

Near the end of August I, and a friend, were passing a card shop in Stillorgan and saw a sign in the window advertising for part time staff. After enquiring about the job and having a lengthy interview with the manager, I was offered the job. The answer to prayer had seemed like it was a long time coming but it was worth the wait. I got the hours I needed, part time morning work, and I would be able to combine it with the children's healthcare regime. I hoped that I would be able to use my annual holidays any time either Emma or Luke had a hospital visit.

The shop was located between our house and the children's school which was perfect. This meant that I would be able to drive them to school and then go to work. They could probably have traveled on the bus but, in the best interests of their health, I chose to drive them to school. I felt it reduced their exposure to infection as they were not on public transport and waiting at cold bus stops. Also if they needed to bring up mucus, it would be less embarrassing to cough that up into tissues in the car instead of on a bus.

I enjoyed learning about the greeting card business and had always had an interest in the different types of cards available. Three of us working at the shop were at similar life stages so we bonded very well from day one. I enjoyed the adult company and meeting the different customers who came into the shop.

In my first week there, I was asked if I would consider being the Assistant Manager. I was thrilled to be asked as I hadn't been too confident about returning to work outside the home and this confirmed to me that I must be doing a good job.

Unfortunately, I had to turn down the offer as I couldn't give it the time or commitment that the position would require, I needed to keep time and energy free to cope with all the demands of the children's health and our daily lives.

Three months into the job, I was routinely collecting Emma and Luke from school one afternoon unaware that our lives were about to change in a moment.

Luke had sent me a text while I was on the way there to say that Emma was crying but she wouldn't tell him why. She wouldn't let him help her either which, naturally, frustrated him. When she got into the car and I asked what was wrong, she said she couldn't breathe. I said I would have to take her to hospital but she pleaded with me not to. She had already had a course of home IV antibiotics in November with trips back and forward to the hospital and she wanted a break from the hospital routine.

The evening of the day that she finished the recent IV course, her cough had returned. This was unusual because normally after her IV's, her health would be better than that and it wouldn't be until nearer the next course of IV's six months later that her health would start to deteriorate again.

The two weeks prior to this she had been awake regularly at night, coughing and generally not feeling great during the day. No-one can understand the CF cough unless they have lived with it. It is a chesty cough and no matter how much mucus they bring up, their body still makes more. The coughing is endless and exhausting.

After what we had been through in the previous couple of weeks and seeing her struggling for breath now, I knew the only place for her was at the hospital. I had been nursing her for 13 years at this point so I knew when she needed to be in hospital for extra treatment and I knew what I could cope with at home. She was adamant that she didn't want to go back to hospital and so the only compromise I could make with her at this stage was that I would go home first, phone the hospital to let them know about her breathing difficulties and see what they advised.. Even in those few minutes of listening to her and trying to reason with her, things changed. She looked at me, with panic in her eyes, and said that if we went home first she did not think she would make it to the hospital alive.

I quickly phoned the hospital on my mobile phone to let them know we were on the way and I explained our emergency to them. Emma had been feeling this way since lunchtime in school but had said nothing. If she had gone to the school nurse, she would have phoned me and I could have collected Emma immediately to bring her to hospital. Then we would have been seen by the CF team who were au fait with all of Emma's treatment and medical history. As it was, by now the team would have gone home for the weekend. The nurse I spoke to on the hospital ward recommended that we go to casualty. She would leave a message with them that Emma was to be seen to immediately. I also sent mobile text messages to family and friends and a prayer chain was started immediately for Emma, Luke and I.

It was a nightmare of a journey. We got stuck in bumper to bumper fog-bound traffic on the road that would lead us to the motorway. I had never seen Emma like this before with fear in her eyes from not being able to breathe properly. I was trying to encourage her to relax as panicking would tighten her airways and make it harder for her to breathe. At times I would turn my head away from her so she couldn't see the tears in my eyes at the thought that we may not make it to the hospital on time. Inside I silently cried out to God for His help.

At one point in the journey I could take no more of this crisis. I was about to phone the police to see if they could help us get through the traffic quicker but then the cars started moving ahead and shortly we were able to get to the motorway that would eventually bring us to the hospital. I was so thankful that the city centre hospital we had been attending had been moved to a new location with better road access and plenty of parking.

When we arrived at the hospital, I parked at the multi-storey car park. Emma did not have enough breath to walk and I did not have time to look for a wheelchair so I put her up on my back and carried her. We did not have time to play with. She was small for her age and anyway at a time of crisis I believe the strength comes from somewhere to do what has to be done.

On hearing that we were having significant traffic problems, the nurse on the ward had got a message to me to say we were to come straight to the ward. They did not say it immediately when we arrived at the hospital but some days later one of the nurses mentioned that the day I had rushed Emma to hospital her lips were turning blue by the time we got to the ward. It had been a traumatic journey but thankfully we had got her to the hospital in time.

Emma was put in the room beside the nurses station and very soon Dr. Ramsey came to see her. I was glad it was him on duty that night because, although he was not on the CF team, he knew some of Emma's health history and was a cheerful person to deal with. He had done cannula resites for Emma and Luke before and always got the needle in the vein first time. She was put on oxygen to help her breathe easier and then Dr. Ramsey took down some details of her recent health. She was also given a Ventolin nebuliser to open the airways.

There were unavoidable delays but finally in the early hours of the Saturday morning she was given her first dose of an antibiotic. At one point of the waiting time I overheard a nurse say 'She looks exhausted' and I realized they were talking about me, not Emma. By then we had had ten hours of crisis, waiting and worry from the time I had collected Emma and Luke from school. Luke and I finally left the hospital at 3am on the Saturday morning when Emma was settled.

Our whole routine changed over the next while as we were spending up to twelve hours at the hospital with Emma each day over the weekend. Her temperature was up which was a sign of infection. Nothing much changed with her condition.

I felt it was important for Luke to keep up the normality of his activities if at all possible. A friend kindly collected him from football practice and then my Dad brought Luke to the hospital later on the Saturday. I would love to have had the energy to plan healthy meals for us to eat at the hospital but the exhaustion meant we were either eating hospital food from the canteen or buying take-away.

To pass the many hours sitting by Emma's bedside, Luke would bring his school homework or watch television or play with the hospital's Playstation. I would watch television or read a magazine. We would talk with each other and if Emma was bored looking at the same four walls, I would take her off the ward for a while.

We had some new things to cope with this time such as Emma being in a wheelchair and on oxygen, she didn't have the breath to walk.

I knew hospital was where Emma needed to be at that time and she was getting the best care available. I continued going to work for the few hours each day and although my manager offered me as much time off as possible, I felt I needed to keep working. That part of the day was one of the things that kept me sane.

Also I knew that with a long term illness, I needed to pace myself. Although her health was bad at that moment, it may get worse and I would need to take time out then. I felt Luke needed his normality of routine as well, even though I'm sure he would have coped very well with days off school.

We had lots of encouragement and support from family, friends and Emma's school teachers. Our minister, Alan, was the first to visit Emma the day after she had been admitted to hospital and kept in regular contact to see how she was doing.

Over the years people have asked what they can do to help. Sometimes there were practical things to do with Luke's routine like helping with school runs. Sometimes there wasn't practical things to help with as so much of their care was hands-on care at any time of the day or night. Always, text messages, phone calls, visits, prayers, support and encouragement were welcome because these showed us we were not alone.

During Emma's first week in hospital, not much changed. Her CF team tried different medications that were new to her usual regime. They also put her on a drip as her potassium and magnesium levels went low. There was still no sign of when she would be coming home as her oxygen levels would have to be stabilized first.

During the first week, Luke got a high temperature. On the Friday when I had rushed Emma to hospital, we didn't have time to collect his nebulisers from home so he had missed out on two doses that day. They did a cough swab and sent it off to the lab to see what infections it was growing. They also did an x-ray to check out what was happening on his lungs. Then an oral antibiotic was prescribed.

At the beginning of Emma's second week in hospital her antibiotics were changed as there had not been sufficient improvement in her condition with the first ones.

Maybe we just desperately needed some hope but it seemed that her health began to improve as soon as she started the new antibiotics. So with that in mind I really wasn't ready to hear what Dr. Greally had to say to me when he phoned the next day.

I always appreciated that he understood the dynamics of our family in that he knew if there was difficult news for Emma, it would be better if he said it to me first and then I could tell her.

The news was not good. Her weight had dropped significantly in the previous ten days as she had lost her appetite. It was a necessity now to put in an nasogastric (NG) tube. I wished there was another way to help her put the weight on. She had been through so much already and having to get this tube in was not going to be easy.

Reluctantly he would allow her home for Christmas but he wanted her back in hospital after that. At home it would be necessary for her treatment to be continued which now included full time oxygen, home IV's administered three times a day plus all her regular treatment of nebulisers three times a day and oral medications. They wanted to do a bronchoscopy at some stage although this would involve Emma going under a general anaesthetic but she was not well enough for this at the moment. A bronchoscopy allows the doctor to visually examine the lower airways through a bronchoscope. They can also take some samples which would be sent to the laboratory to be analysed. The results of the bronchoscopy would give them a more detailed picture of what was happening with her lungs.

To be completely out of Emma's earshot while taking this call, I had gone down the hospital corridor and through the door to a quieter part of the ward away from everyone.

When the phone call was finished, I sat in the dim light and silence of the hospital corridor and cried alone. I had always known it was a terminal illness but somehow when she was well I could push that information to the back of my mind. I could put all my energies into keeping her as well as possible. Now I had to accept that her illness was getting worse, not responding as well to the medications and that some day we may be leaving the hospital without her if she died.

I prayed that God would give me the words to tell Emma what I needed to tell her but first I needed some space to process all the information that had been discussed in the telephone call. So I waited a while longer and then went back to Emma's cubicle.

Typical of any sibling relationship, when I returned to her cubicle it sounded like Emma and Luke were in the middle of a verbal argument. They assured me that this was not them arguing, its the way they communicate. I wanted to talk to Emma alone so I gave Luke some money to spend in the hospital shop and said I would text him when it was time for him to come back into her room. He was very mature in all of this. It must have been difficult for him to have his life turned upside down when she was in hospital. He was too young to be left home alone so every day he had to come to the hospital with me. He just made the best of the situation and never complained about all the attention that she got. All the time he would have been aware that he has the same illness and all this could be ahead for him someday.

I had been trying to avoid eye contact with Emma so she wouldn't see I had been crying but it was not easy to get anything past Emma. When Luke left the room she took one look at my eyes that were obviously still red from crying and asked 'Am I dying?'. I don't think questions get any braver than that. We cried together and I told her she wasn't dying but that they needed to put in an NG feeding tube to help her put weight on.

We talked for a while and then I sent a message to Luke's mobile phone for him to come back into the room. Speaking to them individually meant I could give each of them my full attention to answer any questions they wanted to ask. Although they had appeared to be arguing earlier, underneath it all they looked out for each other and were there for each other when challenging situations arose. When Luke came into the room I talked things through with him and answered his questions.

There was no time to waste as the next day the feeding tube was to be put in. I had taken the day off work so that I could be with Emma while the Registrar, Paul, was putting the tube in. The first two attempts didn't work. Emma was coughing, retching and she turned pink in the face.

Paul left the room to go and talk to Dr. Greally to see if they could give Emma gas to relax her while they were putting in the tube.

While he was out of the room, Emma said she wanted me to tell them that she had decided to not have the feeding tube instead she would just see if the new antibiotics worked. My heart sank, I wished I could make it all better for her and that she would not have to go through the discomfort of having the feeding tube put in.

The reality was though that it was important for her to put on weight so I had to tell her that I was very sorry but I couldn't tell them about her decision not to have the feeding tube. I explained that this was Thursday and if we waited to see if the antibiotic worked it could be early next week before we might see that it wasn't working. Then it would be too late to put the tube in and see an improvement before Christmas. I told her she had been very brave already and had two bad experiences. Then I asked her if she could put those experiences behind her and tell herself that maybe the next one wouldn't be so bad. I also asked her if she would give it another try. She agreed that she would and immediately the nurse went to find Paul. He told Emma that was a very mature thing to do. He had this idea that if I held a cup of water with a straw in it, Emma could sip the water as the tube went down. His suggestion worked and within seconds the tube was in place. Her feeds began at 4.30pm and lasted through the night.

The next five days passed in a flurry of hospital visits and preparing for Emma to come home for a few days at Christmas. Somehow in the middle of all this I managed to do the Christmas shopping for presents. I know at a time like that people didn't expect presents but it gave us some kind of normality and distraction to be preparing to celebrate Christmas.

Emma came home on Christmas Eve that year-my 40th birthday. She was worried that she had spoilt my birthday as she was so unwell and this would mean I had a lot of extra work to do with her healthcare. I reassured her that it was an extra special birthday for me as we had her home with us for Christmas. We had waited until Emma came home to put up the Christmas tree so she could be involved in part of the preparations too.

Unknown to me, Luke had been planning a birthday surprise for the past week. He had organised a special birthday lunch for me at home with my favourite pate and toast, side salad and freshly squeezed orange juice.

For dinner he enlisted his Granny's help to make Chicken a la king with rice earlier that day. He saved up some of his pocket money and had ordered a cake from our local supermarket which was iced with the words 'Happy 40th Birthday Mum'.

I loved every minute of his wonderful surprise and I listened in amazement as he told me how he had planned it all without me knowing.

Family and friends made my birthday special too with lovely text messages, cards, presents and celebrations.

We were encouraged by the continuing thoughtfulness, support and care from friends, family and the teachers, staff and chaplains from Emma and Luke's school. One of the examples of 'going the extra mile' in thoughtfulness that stands out in my mind is when Emma's year leader texted her to say that if she wanted him to shop for presents for Luke and I that would be no problem as he still had his own Christmas shopping to do.

One of the changes I noticed in myself at this time was that because of all the awful moments we had been facing, I was developing a double appreciation for any good moments that came our way.

The next three days I continued with Emma's regime of oxygen, IV antibiotics three times a day, nebulizers three times a day, steroids, oral antibiotics and other medications.

We were allowed to skip the overnight feeds but Emma was to be encouraged to eat as much regular food as possible. She ate very well over Christmas.

It was difficult bringing Emma back to the hospital after having her home for Christmas.

Thankfully she was now responding to the antibiotics and had put on some weight while she was at home so she was able to come home after a week.

Emma had been in hospital for most of the month of December. Previous to this crisis, her medication had always cleared the infections quickly and so I did not have to think too much about CF being a terminal illness. This episode shook me and regularly as I walked along the lonely hospital corridors late at night as I was leaving the hospital to go home, my eyes filled up with tears as I thought of sometime in the future when Emma may die from her illness. This was no longer a thought that I could push to the back of my mind.

9

Life Gets Tougher

Years ago the life span of sufferers of Cystic Fibrosis was often not more than the early teenage years. Nowadays with the advances in medications and treatment they can live longer lives. Side effects of their medications have to be monitored as long term medication can be severe on the body.

When Emma had been in hospital for the month of December they had taken the opportunity to do some tests on her because Dr. Greally was concerned that she had not been growing much over the last while.

We were sent to another hospital for a Dexa scan which is a more detailed x-ray and gives information about bone density. The results came back fairly quickly and unfortunately they showed that she had severe osteoperosis. It's a CF osteoperosis in that it is caused by one of her medications that she absolutely needs to take long term. Thankfully she did not seem to have any symptoms like bones breaking easily or the pain that sometimes goes with osteoperosis. She already had enough to cope with.

When we were at the clinic for Emma and Luke's port flush, Ger found a quiet moment to tell me the results of Emma's Dexa scan. I appreciated that she told me first and that I could then tell Emma later at a more suitable moment.

It sometimes seemed with the CF that it was just one difficult thing after another that we had to cope with. It was only about five weeks after her month long hospital stay that we got this news. I remember commenting to Ger about what a cruel illness CF is. The sufferers can look so well on the outside and yet be deteriorating physically on the inside.

I came away from the clinic, numb, trying to process all my thoughts, feelings and questions on hearing confirmation of the latest development with Emma's health. I felt I owed it to Emma to tell her this news first, after all it was her health. That meant I couldn't talk to anyone else about this for the moment. Also there was a family party coming up on the Sunday for three of us in the family circle who had milestone birthdays to celebrate and I didn't want to spoil the day for anyone, including Emma, by telling them this news beforehand.

I went through the range of emotions, first shock, then disbelief, then extreme tiredness, and then I just felt like I wanted to vomit. It was so unfair, Emma had already been through so much and now this. How could I tell her? As always, I prayed that God would give me the right time and the right words.

Slowly the words formed in my mind and I knew how I would say it to her. Then the right time followed.

We were coming home in the car from school and I asked her would she like to know the test results. She seemed indifferent to knowing them and I said I could leave it till some other time if that was what she wanted. After thinking about it for a moment or two, she decided she would like to know now. Before I told her the results, I said that she needed to remember two things. Firstly, nothing had changed from one day to the next, the results had just highlighted something that had been happening for a while. Secondly, there was medication that would help.

She cried when I told her about the osteoperosis, it broke my heart that she had to face continuing bad news about her health. She had already suffered so much. How much more did she have to take?

When she had finished crying I talked to her about the types of treatment available. One of the medications came in tablet form and the other was an IV. The later can sometimes be painful so the CF team had decided to try the oral medication first. It is a routine medication but the side effects can be extremely severe on the osophesagus.

The CF team were always sensitive to any queries I had about medications and they would talk through those issues with honesty in a helpful way. On this occasion they discussed the guidelines as to how this medication should be taken if adverse side effects were to be avoided. They also discussed what immediate action would be taken if Emma began to show negative side effects. We slotted this new medication into Emma's healthcare regime which seemed to be growing by the minute. She also had to increase her calcium intake in the form of milk, cheese, yogurts, hot chocolate, rice pudding and custard.

Later in this year Emma and Luke both had their routine home IV course of antibiotics. Luke was ok after his course of treatment but Emma's lung function could have been better. She was very upset about this. She was a very intelligent young teenager and knew full well that it was not a good sign if her lung function was down.

When she got her Christmas holidays from school her health went downhill almost immediately as she battled with tiredness and lack of energy. There were three nights at home when I had to encourage her to go on oxygen overnight. On New Years Eve 2004 I drove to the hospital to leave in a sputum sample as I was very concerned about Emma's health.

A few days later, I was very relieved to meet Ger at our local shopping centre. When she asked how Emma was I was able to tell her how bad Emma's health had been over Christmas and she said she would look out for the results of Emma's sputum sample. Ger phoned me two days later to see how Emma was and to say that the full results were not yet through from the lab. I asked if a doctor could review Emma that day as I was very concerned about her breathing. I had been nursing Emma for 16 years and instinct always told me when extra help was needed.

It was awful watching Emma suffer, the endless, persistent and exhausting coughing, bringing up mucus, extra physio needed and her being upset regularly because she felt so awful. She couldn't enjoy her school holidays with all these health issues. The doctor confirmed later that day that Emma had three areas of infection. The good news was that these infections had not been there 6 months earlier so they were treatable. The bad news was that she needed to go on IV's for four or five weeks. So that was the priority of our routine for those next 35 days.

Initially when I had started home IV all those years ago I knew the intensity would only last for two weeks but now this was becoming part of our normal lives. I had to learn how to pace myself for what was ahead. My energy was put into the home IV regime of early mornings, with the first dose at 7am, and late nights with the last dose of IV's finishing at midnight. A lunchtime dose was in between at 3pm.

Emma had side effects of nausea from the antibiotics and she was feeling weak a lot of the time because she was so unwell. I remember her coughing so much during the day and night and bringing up endless amounts of mucus. We had return visits to the hospital for blood tests, needle changes for her port, lung function tests and changes to her antibiotics.

Each day was full of challenges, trying to fit everything in such as the home IV's, necessities like collecting their medicines from the chemist, doing basics like shopping for food, the school run as Emma wanted to go to school so that she did not miss out on too many lessons in her Junior Certificate year, Luke's schooling and his activities like guitar classes.

I was in regular contact with the team who were involved in Emma's care not only at the hospital but also those involved with supplying her oxygen and the company who supplied her antibiotics.

I'm looking back at my notes for this time of our lives and I can't believe I actually kept working through all of this although giving up work was not an option.

The boss very kindly allowed me to change hours when I needed to bring Emma or Luke to hospital but there were times that our routine went into overdrive. There were times when Emma was on a new antibiotic. I would bring her to hospital in the morning before I went to work. She would have her port needled, height and weight checks, and lung function. After this hospital visit I would go to work for a few hours and later that evening I would bring Emma back to hospital for a second dose of antibiotics.

Emma became more private about her health. There were times when she would quietly excuse herself from a social occasion, like dinner with friends, so she could go to the bathroom and cough up mucus. Sometime she would get bursts of energy and want to go shopping. There wasn't many activities she had the energy to do but at least with shopping, she could wander in an out of the shops which might help to lift her mood.

When she got the energy for those moments I would go with the flow knowing how important it was for her to feel some kind of normality. Although these trips always had the potential to turn into a crisis as she didn't have the energy or breathe to walk for long. Sometimes her lips would be turning blue and we would have to take a rest while she calmed her breathing and took some of her inhaler to open up her airways. Sometimes she was able for short outings such as a trip with the hospital to the Pantomime at Christmas.

I had always tried to have mother/daughter, mother/son times with Emma and Luke as they were growing up. As Emma's health deteriorated further our activities were planned at or near home because it felt safer that way. If there was an emergency we were next to the motorway so we could get to the hospital quickly.

Amazingly she did her Junior Certificate exams in school during this year that she was particularly unwell and she got nine honours. Equally amazing, the following year when Luke was watching her being so unwell knowing he had the same illness and that could be ahead for him at some stage, he also did the Junior Certificate exams and got nine honours.

With Emma being on extended courses of IV's for weeks at a time, some of her teachers were concerned about the amount of school she was missing as she had to go home early for the afternoon dose. The school nurse very kindly suggested that I could prepare and administer Emma's 3pm dose of IV's from the nurses station. So that's what I did. I would go straight from work to Emma's school and prepare her medications.

Emma would come out of class and I would give her the flush and start the first antibiotic. She would go back to class and when the antibiotic had gone into her system over half an hour, she would clamp off the line. At the end of class, she would come back to the nurses station where I would flush her line and start the second antibiotic.

Same routine again, back to class and clamp off the line when her antibiotics had gone through. At the end of that class, Emma would come back to the nurses station and I would finish off that dose of treatment. Then we were free to go home. They were awful days but I found that if I tried to settle into the moment rather than fighting it, this gave me a different perspective for coping and I was able to channel my energies into dealing with the daily priorities rather than have my energy evaporate on negative emotions.

During this time as Emma's energy levels got lower she felt she could not continue some of the activities she had been involved in for years. My heart broke for her one day when she made the decision to return a Cup she had won in Girls Brigade. She felt she was no longer able for the energetic routines they practiced and competed in. She loved the social aspect of Girls Brigade so much that she still continued to go there when they met weekly just so she could see her friends and talk with them. When it came to the yearly display, she was invited to sit with the VIP's on the platform to watch the display which I thought was a very special thing for them to do because it meant Emma felt included in the evening.

Over the years I have been very aware that if my health was not good we would have been in a more difficult situation than we already were. Thankfully I had nothing too serious just repeated strep throats, dizzy spells and high cholesterol. As the main carer I didn't have a chance to rest as much as I needed to. At times I would wake up feeling like I was paralysed but I knew that was just the effects of stress.

There was one time when both Emma and Luke ended up in hospital at the same time as they needed IV's for infections. I had to phone the boss the next morning to say 'I don't do sick days, but I cannot physically get out of bed to come to work today'. I had no energy left at that point. Sometimes I would have a short sleep at the hospital while we were waiting for an appointment because I couldn't keep my eyes open any longer.

The exhaustion affected so many parts of my life. There was a physical exhaustion, I just kept going each day regardless of how tired I was because I didn't have options for time out. There was a huge workload each day even with just concentrating on the priorities. There was the emotional exhaustion as we dealt with the deterioration of Emma's health. She was in and out of hospital, her system was not responding to the medication as well as it had in times past. I felt, healthwise, she was beginning to slip away from us.

I find it harder to admit my spiritual exhaustion. I know my faith in God remained firm and I could see how He was providing for us and carrying us through the nightmare. I felt my prayer life was suffering because in the tiredness sometimes I could pray no more than 'Help us God'. There was the mental exhaustion when I felt at times my mind could take no more of the nightmare we were living through.

Emma and I always had the type of relationship where we could talk about anything. In the hospital as part of the team there are psychologists and social workers who would be there if Emma wanted to talk through anything. However she would always say to them 'It's ok I can talk to my Mum about everything'. Because of the nature of the illness we were dealing with, those talks were sometimes very intense. Emma would confide in me that she thought she was dying. She would say that her system was getting used to the antibiotics and that's why they didn't seem to be working. We would talk this through until she had exhausted all the thoughts stressing her.

At the end of this particular IV course which lasted 35 days Emma was taken off the antibiotics not because she was any better but because the infection was not responding to the medicine. The doctors wanted to give Emma's system a bit of a break from the antibiotics and also wanted a chance to consider what the next step would be.

After the two weeks I was told that Dr. Greally would like an appointment with me. I really appreciated the relationship that we had built over the years with the CF team we had come to know and trust.

Ger had dropped the word transplant into a conversation we had the week before I was to meet with Dr. Greally. She didn't say that was what he wanted to talk about. However, the very fact that she had mentioned the word meant it went round in my head for days and I was able to think about what questions I would ask him if he were to bring up the subject. I believe this was God preparing me for what I would hear at the meeting.

I didn't ask anyone to come with me to the appointment. There had been so many times in the previous years when I had to face things alone but I didn't feel alone because I could pray and believed God was always with me. Also I have a great support network of friends and family. I knew the day I was going to see the Consultant that they would be praying for me and they were there for me when I needed them.

I had been honest with Emma and told her I was going to a meeting with Dr.Greally. She knew that when I came home I would talk to her about whatever he had said. When I was sitting in the meeting that day I had this huge sense of peace surrounding me. It was like as if a shield was all around me and it was protecting me from the awfulness of what I had to hear about Emma's deteriorating health.

I was so exhausted with all we had been through in the previous eighteen months as her health had become progressively worse. She had frequently needed oxygen overnight, had needed IV's more often and for longer periods of time, was regularly awake in the early hours of the morning coughing up mucus and being upset about her health. Her medicine was not as effective as it had been previously. The CF team had been fantastic. They were always there for us, encouraging us and supporting us. I knew I just had to pick up the phone and there would be someone there to help when we needed it.

Dr. Greally started the meeting by asking me how I thought Emma was doing healthwise. I replied to his question by answering honestly and saying that I felt she was slipping away from us. He confirmed that they, the CF team, had noticed a deterioration in her health over the previous 18 months. She had not responded well to medication and when they see that pattern beginning, now would be the time to start considering a double lung transplant. We had a window of opportunity of two years.

He was open and honest in his answers to every question I had. He explained what the procedure would be if Emma decided to go down the transplant route. It would have to be her decision as she would be the one who would need to put the effort into her recovery.

We would have to go over to Newcastle in England for an assessment to see if she was a suitable candidate for transplantation. Then there would be the waiting time to see if she got onto the transplant list. There appears to be a very fine line for getting on the waiting list. The patient has to be ill enough to be put on the list but well enough to survive the operation. A double lung transplant would give Emma a different quality of life but she would have to take anti-rejection drugs for the rest of her life. She would still have the CF in her digestion and she would still have CF osteoperosis. There were certain things going against her like her osteoperosis and poor nutrition, as her appetite was often not good when she had infections. Her petite size also was against her. Although she was fifteen years old she was the size of a twelve year old and lungs of that size had not been available in the past year.

We had been thinking about a holiday to Greece with my parents but this was now out of the question. On hearing this latest development in Emma's health, I would not take the chance of going on holiday. If we were to go, Emma would need oxygen on the flight and possibly in the apartment as well. Her low lung function would make her prone to bad chest infections. If she got an infection while we were in Greece, she would have to be flown to the mainland for treatment. If she were admitted to a foreign hospital for treatment, we would be dealing with someone who did not know her medical history. All things considered, that would not be a holiday, it would be a nightmare. So those plans had to be put on hold or shelved altogether.

Dr. Greally ended the meeting by leaving it up to me to talk to Emma about transplant. It would be her decision as to whether or not she wanted to choose the transplant route. Her answer was needed as soon as possible as they would have to plan the next course of action.

When Dr. Greally left the room that day, I felt I had asked all the questions that I wanted to ask at that stage and they had been answered thoroughly. I believe all the prayers surrounding me that day protected me and kept me clear minded so that I would be able to think about relevant questions I needed to ask.

Jenny, one of the CF nurses, said I had been very brave with the way I had handled all that I had just heard about Emma's health. I did have a small cry then but I am a private person so I kept most of my crying for later when I left the hospital.

I cried most of the way home. I wanted to talk to someone but I felt so lost that I didn't know who to go to. Anyway, this was Emma's news and she deserved to hear it first so that it would give her time to decide what she wanted to do. Our Church is about 5 minutes away from where we live. I sat in my car in the church car park and cried till the tears dried up. I needed some space to process all the information and to deal with all the emotions.

How do you tell your teenage daughter her health is so bad she needs to make a decision that will affect whether she lives or dies? Life was so unfair. We should be fighting about her wanting to go out to discos or stay out late with her friends and any other teenage issues. Anything but this.

How does anyone make a decision about transplant anyway? On the one hand, if she didn't have it, she would most certainly die. On the other hand, if she did have the transplant she would have a new quality of life but some of the CF problems would still be there. While CF rumbles along getting progressively worse, post-transplant would be an acute situation. Also the anti-rejection drugs would be toxic to her system. She would still have CF in her digestion, CF diabetes and CF osteoperosis. There was so much to take into consideration in making a major decision like this.

After crying I couldn't go home straight away so I went to get some take-away for dinner. I imagined that by the time I had done that my eyes would not be red from crying anymore and I could go home.

As I had done in all the other difficult times so far I prayed that God would give me the words to talk to her and the right time to say it. It was such a huge issue to talk about and I felt it might be better if we had some mother/daughter time over a meal to discuss things. However that was not meant to be.

Later that evening Emma was in her bedroom and when I went up to see if she was ok, she asked what Dr. Greally had discussed with me. I sat on the bedroom floor beside her.

She listened intently while I told her everything he had said. She had lots of questions so together we talked through the information in the transplant booklet they had given me earlier in the hospital. We sat together on the floor and cried, it was heartbreaking.

Up to that point we had always discussed things together but his time I noticed a change in her. She was now beginning to own her illness. In a maturity way beyond her years, she said she needed some time to think. It was so hard to walk out of her bedroom and give her the space she needed to think this through. I wanted to be there for her in this most awful time of her life but I had to respect her need for space. I went down to the kitchen and as I washed the dishes, I prayed that God would wrap His loving arms around her and protect her mind as she thought through this minefield of information to reach a decision.

The following morning Emma told me that she would be interested in going on the transplant list. She just had some questions about post transplant life that she needed the team to answer before giving her final decision.

Ger hadn't been at the meeting when Dr. Greally spoke with me but she phoned me two days later to see how I was doing after hearing all that had been said. I appreciated that about Ger, she always went the extra mile in her care and support taking into account the whole family unit. She discussed with me in more detail some of the things that had been mentioned at the meeting.

Emma's weight had been a concern for a long time and although we had been able to avoid having a PEG feeding tube put in, now it would be a necessity to bring Emma's weight up to an acceptable level for a transplant operation.

Also to have Emma's lungs in the best possible condition, she would need to go on a 12 week course of IV's.

The IV course was scheduled to start at the end of April. The morning we were to go to the hospital to have Emma's port needled to start the IV course, Luke got stomach cramps. Emma was started on her IV's and the next few days I had to keep an eye on Luke also as he was given new medication to help with the pains in his stomach. He also had a temperature and needed regular paracetamol to help bring this down.

During this time, Emma was introduced to a new physio device called an Acapello. The way it works is that the plastic mouthpiece is placed in the mouth. The patient breathes slowly into the device and their breath causes a see-saw effect inside the device which in turn causes the mucus to be loosened on their chest. They are then able to cough up the mucus so that it is not sitting on their lungs becoming infected and causing more scarring with each infection. This was a breakthrough in Emma's physiotherapy regime.

She could watch television while she was doing this and so she didn't mind doing the physiotherapy for an hour at a time which was very effective.

Luke was also introduced to the Acapello a while later and it proved to be the most effective physiotherapy for him too. It gave them both the independence to do their own physio rather than them feeling I had to do it all the time for them.

Things had been extremely challenging and difficult for us all in previous eighteen months. We were already exhausted and now there was more ahead. Exactly what was ahead we did not know and maybe it was better that way. If we knew what was ahead we might have been overwhelmed but this way we would be taking it a step at a time.

I was looking back on my Encouragement Book for this time and was extremely thankful for the support and encouragement our friends and family gave us. We had an army of people praying for us. Friends and family kept in touch by phone calls, emails and text messages. Those closest to me would listen if I needed to talk or sometimes they recognized I needed some space to digest difficult information I had heard about Emma's health. Emma and Luke's school went the extra mile in their caring particularly Emma's year leader, form teacher, home economics teacher, library assistant, nurses and chaplaincy team. The hospital team were amazing too. They were always there at the end of the phone when I needed to discuss, or had a concern about, Emma's health issues.

Before one particular Bank Holiday weekend, Ger phoned to make sure everything was ok with Emma and Luke. I was impressed with her thoughtfulness. I was also encouraged by comments that came from the CF team. I was just doing my best, with God's help, to get through the crisis but I was encouraged to hear the CF team's comment that they 'constantly marvel about how I manage to cope with everything'.

Emma, Luke and I worked well together as a team, encouraging each other.

My relationship with God was changing and deepening at this time. I tried to have my quiet time each day because this kept me centered for whatever I had to face that day. The days I struggled more were those when I didn't have that quiet time. I also noticed that my prayer life was changing as there were so many moment by moment prayers needed as we faced constant health issues.

Many years before this God had become everything to me in a time of crisis. It was a comfort to look back on those days and see that He had been faithful in helping me through the awfulness. I knew that God who had been true and faithful to us in the past would continue to do so in our present situation. I would find this knowledge and previous experience a comfort in the months to come as our situation became more extreme.

10

The Transplant Route

I accepted that it was Emma's decision to choose the transplant route and I was committed to giving her 100% support.

I also believed that God is a powerful God and if He would just say the words she would be healed. I constantly reminded Him of that. I spent many hours thinking over the different types of healing. I knew that if God took Emma to Heaven she would be healed immediately and completely. On the other hand, the transplant would restore quality of life to her and she would still be with us but she would still have some of the complications of CF and some new complications that would come with the after care of the transplant.

Emma knew that at any time she could pull out of the transplant process if that was her decision. However, for the moment we were in the process of preparation heading towards transplant if the organs became available. To give Emma the best chance of surviving a transplant operation she needed have a higher body mass index (BMI). Her weight had always been an issue. She was underweight and it was a constant struggle for her to put on weight no matter how much she ate. At times the infections would rob her of her appetite and it was even more of a losing battle to try to keep weight on her. So in mid Summer a date for a PEG feeding tube operation was scheduled. The night before Emma was to have this op, some friends came over to our house to pray about the day ahead of us and Emma's PEG operation. I was glad of the support from everyone there because it filled me with the sense that we were not alone in all of this.

Emma's health was fragile at this stage. In the pre-theatre room, the next day, there were complications and she ended up on a ventilator.

She did come around after two hours and I was allowed to go down and see her in the recovery room where she was linked up to all sorts of machines to monitor her. She felt her stomach and being a bit drowsy from the anaesthetic she mumbled, 'I can't feel the tube.' I explained to her that the operation had not gone ahead.

It always amazed me how well she was able to bounce back after her health plummeting. That night in the high dependency unit, she was obviously feeling recovered from her earlier ordeal, she sat up in bed and asked me if I thought she would be well enough to get out of hospital at the weekend to take part in the car boot sale at our Church.

I was drained by the earlier experience but not wanting to take away her hope I said we would see how things went. I wished someone would link me up to an IV to give me a burst of energy, I was shattered by now. She didn't make it to the car boot sale as she spent the next six days in hospital. However, she was very much part of the experience as we kept in touch by text messages all the time.

I noticed, from the time when Emma was very little, that she had a great energy for life. It was as if she realized that maybe her life was going to be shorter and she wanted to make the best of the life she would live.

By now we were back to that routine of rearranging our lives around her hospital routine. I was spending 7-10 hours with Emma each day. Luke was getting older now and he didn't always want to spend hours sitting in her room at the hospital. He was keeping reasonably well at this stage. He still had the routine of daily medicine and physiotherapy, monthly port flushes, three monthly clinic visits, twice yearly home IV's and the yearly Annual Assessment. While Emma was in hospital this time, Luke wanted to enjoy normal activities for his school summer holidays. So he attended a soccer camp, played computer games and spent time with his friends.

When I look back on those days I realise that, physically it must have been adrenelin that kept me going. My stress and tiredness levels went into overdrive. This is an extract from a journal I wrote in now and then as we went through our experiences...

7th June 2005...I felt like giving up again today - it's all a bit too much. Emma had an eye test at the hospital from 10.30 until 12 noon. Then Luke had a 12 noon appointment to have his IV's started. He is to stay on his morning and evening nebulisers and we were given the details about his home IV antibiotics. The lung function test results were lower than usual and an x-ray showed some changes. Their appointments took longer than I expected so I phoned work to rearrange my work hours for today. We got out of the hospital at 1.15 and after stopping at a shop to get some rolls for lunch, I went into work till 6.15pm....Mad mad day and it didn't get much better the next day. As I had done my short day in work yesterday I had to work until 2pm today. Emma started the day off with bringing up a load of mucus and then became very upset and was crying and moaning. (She was understandably exhausted fighting her illness but the crying would block her airways).

I was up at 7am to start the IV's on both Emma and Luke. We were finished the IV at about 8am and then I brought Emma to school to do her first Junior Certificate exam. She was very tired. I texted her on my mobile phone at break time and later she texted back to ask if I could collect her outside the nurses station. She didn't have the energy or breath to walk the short distance to the sports centre car park When I collected her, her eyes were reddish around the eyelids and her breathing wasn't great. When we got home I started the IV's for both Emma and Luke. Later I drove Luke to the local park to watch his friend play in a football match.

Emma and I went to the supermarket to get salad and meat. Emma stayed in the car because she had no energy for walking. Then it was home and set up Emma's second IV.

Eat the salad we had just bought for lunch. Collect Luke from the park, home again....I was quite frightened to see Emma because she was sitting on the floor leaning up against a pillow on the bed and she was half asleep linked up to the oxygen. She said she can't go on like this. I suggested that we start her nebuliser, give her the night time medicines and she could go to bed early to get some rest. She had had a late night last night and a stressful day today...With the exhaustion of the effort of breathing she often get times when she cries and moans and can't calm down. She wanted her inhaler but it would not have done much good while she was so upset because she was blocking her airways. In the end when she calmed down she didn't need her inhaler.'

This would have been what we were living through daily at this point. We were trying to keep some kind of normality to our lives but we were also living with the daily crisis of Emma's health getting worse. She wanted to go to school and do her exams but to be honest I was often amazed at how she got through the day. The effort of breathing while her lungs were in such a bad state was enough to be concentrating on for the whole day let alone trying to also do her studies. She really was an inspiration to see how she coped with the demands of each day.

A few months prior to Emma ending up in hospital after her PEG op, I had set a date for a family meal to celebrate Mum and Dad's 45th wedding anniversary. I didn't know at the time that Emma would be in hospital. We asked permission for Emma to be allowed out of hospital for a few hours so she could be part of the celebrations. Emma's consultant had given the ok for this earlier in the day.

I noticed that Emma was losing confidence in being outside the four walls of the hospital. She felt safer within the confines of the hospital knowing the very best help was available. It was lovely to have the family together that night for the meal but from Emma's health viewpoint, stress was served on a plate. When we left the hospital to go to the meal, we traveled along the motorway. Before we got to the toll bridge, Emma was feeling unwell. I knew she was just panicking so I encouraged her to take the evening a moment at a time...we would try getting to the hotel...then we would try getting through the starter...then we would try getting through the main course…then the dessert…then the chat. I told her if she felt at any point that she needed to go back to the hospital that was all right. So I spent the whole meal, waiting and watching, preparing for a mad dash back along the motorway. Although it was difficult to bring Emma back after the meal, I think we were both a bit relieved that there had been no major crisis that night.

We were so blessed by the support and encouragement during her hospital stay. I am looking back at my encouragement book for those days, here are some of the wonderful words of encouragement that lifted our spirits…we will keep you in our prayers, do not forget to call if you need anything…I am praying God will give you the strength to keep going…Your workplace is a hotline of prayer…there is much prayer for the three of you and people all over the world have you covered in prayer…thoughts and prayers are with you all today…It's tough, am sure, hang in…am not busy, this is VIP and want to support as best I can…If you need to chat at any time of the day or night just call…Give us a shout if we can help out. Emma is a tough cookie, as is her Mum…If there is anything I can do let me know, a meal? transport for Luke? Shopping?

Encouragement in these tough days lifted my spirit and let me know that we were not alone.

It was vital for the feeding tube to be inserted so the operation was rescheduled.

In the month before this operation we had booked into a family holiday in an adventure centre in Co. Wicklow. I know it probably does not sound ideal given our circumstances with Emma's health but we would be with friends and were not too far from Dublin if we needed to rush back to hospital. The children would have a programme of activities for their age group that they could take part in if they wanted to and I would have plenty of adult company.

It was the kind of holiday where you can drive to it, park the car and you don't have to do any driving for the rest of the week. I'm reading this and thinking how did we consider going on this holiday but I know that we were all exhausted and badly needed to get away for a change of scene.

Emma had been awake almost every night of the previous week coughing up mucus. One night she was awake for an hour because her breathing was shallow. That same day Luke had problems breathing but the wheeziness disappeared when he had some medicine in his nebuliser.

At this stage of Emma's illness it was necessary to bring the oxygen compressor with us on the week's holiday. It is said that this compressor is portable but all that means is that it is on wheels. The unit itself is heavy and it took Luke and I lots of energy to lift it into the back seat of the car. With the unit strapped with a seat belt we started out on our journey.

We were merrily on our way when suddenly Emma opened the window and stuck her head out. When I asked her what she was doing, she told me she was trying to breathe. Emma's survival instincts were always strong; she had seen a pub along the way and wanted me to go back to ask the owner if we could plug in her oxygen compressor. This was turning into a nightmare. She said if she did not have oxygen she would probably not be alive by the time we reached our destination. I realized this episode was just part of the panic that was beginning to set into her as her health deteriorated. I tried to talk to her to keep her calm but it was not working. So in the end I had to tell her that I needed to stop talking to concentrate on our journey as I wasn't entirely sure of the route we were to take. This was true. When we arrived at the adventure centre, the first thing we did was set up the oxygen compressor for Emma. She didn't really need it by then but I thought it would settle her a bit to have some oxygen anyway.

We had a lovely week with friends. Emma wasn't able for a lot of the activities planned for her age group but she got involved with some of the activities. At times when she wasn't able to walk up the steep driveway, I and plenty of others took turns to help carry her. The illness was robbing us of so much but we were equally determined to claim back as many happy times as we could. These would stand to us in the tough times that were ahead. I noticed that this holiday had come just before we were heading into a crisis. I often looked back and thought of how this holiday was God's provision for us because He knew of what was ahead for us.

11

Second Try

Emma's PEG tube operation was scheduled for the end of August. In order for her lungs to be in the best possible condition for the operation, she needed a week of home IV's beforehand. I was back into the routine of early mornings and late nights as the doses were at 7am 3pm and 11pm. Emma was able to sleep through the first and last dose so in this way she was able to get the rest she needed. We had return visits to the hospital for blood tests.

I was very worried about this PEG operation after what had happened previously. Her 16th birthday was coming up the first week in September and I arranged a surprise party for her a week early which was also the night before her operation. I invited family, some of Emma's friends and lots of people who had been supportive and encouraging to us in times of crisis. I wanted happy memories of that night to remain with us. Also I believed it would be good for Emma to have her mind occupied with happier thoughts the night before going into hospital. A friend did the catering and the atmosphere in the hall that night was lovely.

We checked into the hospital the following day. She didn't really settle well, it was darker, older and noisier than the hospital she was used to. She cried in my arms the night before the operation and wanted me to ask the doctors to cancel it. I wished for her sake that she did not have to go through so many horrible experiences with her health. As best I could, I tried to explain to her how necessary this operation was.

Our CF team had discussed potential problems with this team so it was decided to put her asleep with gas this time. She was allowed to hold the mask over her mouth and nose. Later I commented on how strong the human instinct is. As she became more drowsy, she kept trying to take the mask away. At one point I could no longer hold the mask in place because she was too strong for me so the anaesthetist took over. Here I was again facing the moment that I always found so hard, leaving her there when she was out cold.

Emma cried coming out of the anaesthetic. She was very thirsty and complained of not being able to breathe. She kept muttering a word and when we eventually understood what she was saying, it turned out to be the name of her usual hospital. She wanted to go back there immediately where she knew the doctors and nurses and everything was familiar.

Her blood sugars were checked regularly. She was put on IV fluids and was also on oxygen and two nebulisers. Her IV antibiotics were continued. Two days later she was allowed to go back to her usual hospital for the recovery period.

Emma was in hospital for another week so I was back into the routine that was fast becoming the norm for us. Emma spent her 16th birthday in hospital. I was glad we had had the party the week before because we had special memories of that. On the day of her birthday, the nurses and playroom staff surprised

Emma with a cake, present and they sang 'Happy Birthday' to her. It was so thoughtful that they were trying to make her day special.

When I was going home from hospital that night, I cried all the way home with emotional and physical exhaustion. I had written what I call a modern Psalm two days before this.

In the Bible I love that the Psalms are so honest. They tell God exactly how the author is feeling about whatever he is going through but always comes back to the goodness of God's character. You will be glad to know that it's shorter than Psalm 119, which has 176 verses.

A Modern Psalm

How much longer, Lord. I want to run but you placed my feet firmly in this place. I can't understand how our present difficulties would be you will for us. You are a God of love...and I'm not challenging that love, I'm just trying to make sense of what we are going through.

I love order but our situation robs us of the opportunity to live an ordered life. So we persevere with the battle between the important things that need to be done versus the order we would want for our lives.

I am robbed of energy by tiredness and so I live the frustration of the dishes piling up, the car needing to be tidied and washed, the garden needing to be tended, the ironing needing to be done and the house needing to be cleaned, letters need to be sent and bills need to be paid. There is so much to be done but the hours are swallowed up by the endless hours in the hospital and the care of her illness.

There is a book to be written, a course to be studied, a healthy lifestyle to be lived, family times to be enjoyed, fun to be had. But it is a huge effort to carve out time for these things as our lives slip away consumed with the demands of each day.

Lord, we have looked to you for so long, you are our only hope. We can't live our lives like this, Lord. Isn't suffering supposed to be just for a season?

Lord, we love her and she is so brave...she has suffered for so long...we cry out to you for healing.

Why is this going on so long?

Is it my fault...is there some lesson I keep missing and I have to be kept in this place till I learn it?

Lord, thank you that you have never given up on me even in those times when I had given up on myself. Thank you for persevering.

I'm trying so hard to see you in all of this, Lord, but it's breaking my broken heart watching her deteriorate before my eyes.

Thank you Lord, that you are with me in my darkest hours when I am all alone and everything seems black.

You promise me a partner to share my life with and I wait endlessly enduring the loneliness.

It's so hard to wait, needing this blessing now, Lord, watching what I see as the best years passing me by. I don't understand it Lord. I come to you disillusioned in the time of waiting and I cry out to you and you quietly and calmly say 'Desolation will be a thing of the past'. Is it too much to ask, Lord, when will that be?

I'm struggling, Lord, because I feel so alone in all of this. I don't know who to turn to and you seem so far away. I want so much more of you in my life, is this your way to bring me into a deeper relationship with you...revealing more of yourself through my struggles? I'm tired, Lord, isn't there an easier or shorter way?

Help me, Lord, because too many times recently I have felt that I just can't persevere anymore...I just can't live like this, with so much pain, heartache and suffering... and yet I don't want to give up on you, Lord, because one thing I know for sure is that without you my life is nothing. Every time I feel like quitting, Lord please strengthen me and sustain me, help me not to give up.

In this time of struggle help me to remember all that you have brought me through so far and how you have become my Strength, my Prince of Peace, my Faithful Provider, my Closest Friend, my Hiding Place, my Comfort, my Counsellor, my God of restoration, my Deliverer, my God of the Impossible, my God for Whom Nothing is Too Hard, my Hope in Times of Trouble, my Light in the Darkness, my Fortress, my Rock, my Reason for Living. You are everything to me, Lord, I don't ever want to be without you.

Emma was in the hospital for the next week but the day she was allowed home she said she was not feeling the best. Her breathing was not good. She also had a headache and a pain in her back. We had her home with us for just over a day and then she deteriorated further. I tried giving her extra oxygen as that sometimes helped but on this occasion it didn't work. It was a stressful journey to the hospital because I was not sure if we would make it in time.

There was no wheelchair at the car park and I could not leave her alone while I went to find one. Every few steps towards the A+E department Emma would stop walking and bend over. When I asked her to try to keep going she said she couldn't breathe enough to walk so I picked her up in my arms and walked as quick as I could to get her into the hospital. I still remember the panic of those moments. I didn't know if I was going to be able to carry her that far but I had to try. The children always used to tease me for being physically strong, like the time I was trying to dig up the root of a small tree in the garden and I snapped the handles of three garden spades in the process. I didn't know the way to the Children's A+E but it just seemed that when people saw me carrying her, they pointed in the right direction and helpfully opened doors to allow us to get us where we needed to be.

Emma's oxygen saturation had dropped way below acceptable levels which was not a good sign at all. She was feeling terrible and told me that she thought this was it, she felt she was going to die that night. It was frightening to see her so critically ill but I had to try to keep positive for her sake. I told her that she wasn't going to die that they would give her oxygen and whatever else she needed to help her breathe better.

Shortly they transferred her to the High Dependency Unit to keep an eye on her overnight. I slept in a chair beside her bed. I was so exhausted. The next day I went home to get some of her things to bring to the hospital. Mum and Dad looked after Luke for the day at their house and brought him back to our house later that night.

Later in the day Emma was transferred from HDU to what was lovingly referred to as her room. She was spending so much time in the hospital that there was a particular room on the ward that she was put into if it was available. We were back to living in a crisis situation.

I was traveling between home and hospital, trying to keep the household running as smoothly as possible and more importantly trying to keep the three of us together so that our family togetherness did not deteriorate.

Luke's health was never as bad as Emma but there were times that he had to be in hospital for treatment for an acute infection or unexpected treatment.

In the week following Emma being readmitted to hospital, she got the results of her Junior Certificate exam. I was so proud of her when I heard that she got 9 honors. That same day Luke was taken into hospital as he had an acute infection that needed some IV treatment. Ideally, with CF, when they are in hospital they should not share a room or a ward with anyone else as this exposes them to infection. Emma was in room number 8 and Luke was next door in room number 7. Luke did not like staying in hospital but I think he drew some comfort from the fact that Emma was in the room next to his. Although they were very funny about it because neither of them wanted to go into each others room in case they caught each other's infection so one would stand at the door of the other's cubicle to talk.

I couldn't go into work the next day as I was physically sick with exhaustion. I phoned the boss and explained that Luke was now in hospital. She said that she didn't know how I was still standing with all we were going through so to take a few days if I needed it. I took two days off. I had always tried to get to work every day that I was rostered on even if it meant that sometimes I would go straight from the hospital to work. Also I felt that in work I was part of a team and I didn't want to let that team down by taking time off.

Luke was in hospital for five days and then he was discharged for me to continue the IV's at home. That day I was also trained in how to work a new portable oxygen unit for Emma. Her deteriorating health now demanded that she carry oxygen with her wherever she went.

I look back on this time and I can't believe how I coped with the physical workload we had each day. I believe my faith in God gave me the strength, wisdom, hope and a peace that passes all understanding for everything that we had to face each day. He surrounded us with a network of loving, praying friends.

For the rest of the month I took a minute at a time as I coped with the routine of Emma staying in hospital and Luke on his home IV's. We got Emma home for a week at one stage but she had to go back into hospital after that as she couldn't breathe. I noticed that each time Emma's health deteriorated further she began to feel safer in the hospital where the doctors and nurses knew her healthcare inside out.

With Emma's health deteriorating further our house became filled with more of her necessary medications and trying to keep these out of sight so Emma and Luke were not constantly reminded of the medications they needed was impossible. I had their oral medications in a press but their IV medications and supplies were on the top of a sideboard. Her oxygen compressor, night time feeding machine and her nebulizer were all in her bedroom. We had a tube connected to the oxygen compressor and going all the way down the stairs to wherever Emma was at any given time.

It was a tough time for all of us. Luke wouldn't often talk about what we were facing but now and then he would say something that let me know that he thought deeply about our situation. One time he passed a comment to me that showed me how he had noticed that Emma's health had gone downhill rapidly within a two year period and, in the back of his mind, he wondered if that could happen to him too. Generally though he kept quite positive. He has always had a placid nature and after facing a difficulty he would leave it behind as he faced the next moment.

Emma always had an inbuilt strength to face her health issues but it was only natural that as her health deteriorated there were times that she said she felt like giving into her Cystic Fibrosis. At times she said the only thing that kept her going was me.

Her faith was very important to her too but it upset her sometimes that she had so many questions about why God would allow her suffering. I told her that was the sign of an active, healthy faith. I reasoned that if her faith were dead she would not bother questioning.

I look back at the things I have written in my encouragement book for that time and I know we were so blessed to have the support of friends and family. I didn't feel alone because at just the right time a text message would arrive at my phone or someone would offer to help with Luke's routine. It meant so much to know that people were praying for us and thinking about us. There were still a lot of difficulties ahead.

12

Our First Trip to Newcastle

In September 2005 we got a call to go to the city centre hospital in Dublin to see the Lung Transplant team that had come over from Newcastle in England. We hoped at that meeting they would give some indication as to whether or not she would be well enough to go on the waiting list.

The morning of the meeting I administered Luke's home IV's at the 7am dose (Flush, antibiotic for half an hour, flush, second antibiotic for half an hour, flush,) and this would have finished about 8am. After that I disconnected Emma from her overnight feeding machine, brought her the medicine for her nebulisers and also her oral medications before we set off for her midday appointment.

At the meeting she needed to get the point across that she was really up for the transplant. She really wasn't in the mood to talk to the doctors and some of her answers to their questions may not have seemed too positive. Anyway the result of that meeting was that they asked if we would go to Newcastle for Emma to be assessed. Emma agreed that she would and after that it was a matter of waiting for the next available appointment which actually came about two weeks later.

My friends Fern and Bruce, whom I have known from my youth club days, and who attend the same church as us had said to me that if and when we were called to Newcastle Luke could stay with them. Often over the time that Emma's health was deteriorating, Fern would have a cup of tea made for me at her house late at night as I was coming home from the hospital. We would sit and chat and she would listen anytime I needed to talk about Emma's health worries. It was such a blessing that they had offered to mind Luke when Emma was called to Newcastle for assessment because I knew he would settle into their family environment well. He was in youth club with their two daughters and knew the family very well. Their house was not too far from ours so it meant Luke could spend his time between our house and theirs. Also, Emma's Year Leader from her school had offered to help out with lifts to and from school as he lived in the area near us. This meant that Luke would be kept in a familiar routine which would be important at this time of crisis.

The morning we were to go to Newcastle an ambulance collected us from the hospital. They took us to the runway at Dublin Airport where there was a small six seater plane waiting.

Emma was too unwell to travel at the higher altitudes which made it necessary for us to travel by chartered flight.

When we arrived at Newcastle Airport an ambulance was waiting to take us to the hospital.

Over the next day or so the tests which involved lung function and walking did not go so well as Emma did not have the energy or the breath for them. The Consultant met with us after a couple of days to say that she was too unwell to go on the list. He had some recommendations to make to her treatment but he didn't think things would improve much. I had nursed

Emma for 16 years and I knew how desperate things were now. In a quieter moment away from Emma, I asked a direct question and the honest answer confirmed what I knew in my heart anyway, she possibly only had a few months left to live.

My faith in God gave me the courage and the strength to face this awful reality. The hope that the transplant route offered was not going to be a reality for us yet.

The next day we traveled back to Dublin. It was sad to be coming home from this assessment knowing that her health was so bad that at this point nothing much could be done for her. When we arrived back in Dublin we were brought straight from the Airport runway to the hospital. It felt like our lives were turning into a war zone with all the crisis of 24 hour care.

The room at the hospital was now becoming like a second home to Emma as she spent so much time there. The nurses and the CF team were all becoming like family to us. I remember one night, when I had to bring Emma back to the hospital for care, asking her if she minded spending so much time there. She just shrugged her shoulders and in a resigned tone said she didn't really think about it anymore, it was just something that had to be done. She was so brave and accepting of her health issues.

We spent so much time at the hospital. Late one night when I was leaving to go home, I asked the security man if he would open the doors, which had been locked for security purposes. He smiled and asked if I had forgotten my swipe card. He thought I was staff who worked at the hospital because he had seen me there so often.

Our minister and friend, Alan, was the first to visit Emma in hospital the day after we came home from Newcastle. He was a great support during this tough time we were going through and I often thought about how he was a God-send. He had started his term in our Church the year Emma's health started to deteriorate and over the next years of crisis that we went through his pastoral care was such a blessing.

The following week I requested a meeting with one of the Consultants from Emma's team, Dr. Basil. I wanted to ask him the same question I had asked the Consultant in Newcastle about how long he thought Emma had left to live. His opinion agreed with the other consultant.

We had had so much bad news to tell people about Emma's health for so long and it got to the point that although I needed the support of family and friends, I struggled with telling them more bad news. I became very selective in who I told our news to and began telling people less because I didn't want to upset them.

I had booked Emma, Luke and I places on the October weekend away with the church Mum and Dad attended. When the time came around, Emma was too unwell to go. The weekend would take place in Waterford which was a few hours of a drive away from Dublin. I would not feel happy having her that far from home, as she was now critically ill, knowing that if we had an emergency with her health we would have to go to a local hospital who would be unfamiliar with her case. So Luke and I discussed it and made the decision that he would still go to the weekend. His Granny and Grandad would bring him there in their car and they would keep an eye on him for the weekend.

I was disappointed that our present crisis was separating the family but I was later to realise that this situation was also preparing Luke. In the future there would be a time when I had to be away from him because of Emma's health but I would know, and he would know, that he would be ok because he would be surrounded by the love and care of family and friends.

In October 2005 Emma was starting her second full month in hospital. Two of the recommendations Newcastle had made were added to Emma's increasing healthcare routine. One was the Bipap breathing machine which would help her breathing when she was asleep and the other was Insulin. She had been borderline diabetic but the night time feeds through her feeding tube meant she now needed a small daily dose of Insulin. We were shown how to use the Insulin pen and after practicing on oranges we were able to give Emma her first dose.

I remember the first night she used the Bipap breathing machine. It was a compact machine with a tube leading from it to the mask that covered her mouth and nose. The settings on the machine are specific to each patient so, Keith, from the oxygen company set it up for Emma. If there were any changes to be made, the Consultant would contact Keith to come and change the settings.

Up to now when Emma and I said our goodnights, she may have something else she wanted to talk about. Now it was a bit more difficult as wearing the mask made her voice muffled. I know we could have taken the mask off but sometimes it took a while for her to feel it comfortable on her face. She was so brave, so accepting that this was just the next part of her treatment that she needed.

It upset me to see her lying there at night time linked up to this machine which was necessary to help her breathe and also to be linked up to the oxygen. I wanted her to have a normal life and not to have to cope with all the awfulness, limitations and deteriorations of her health.

The support from the CF team at the hospital was fabulous. Dr. Greally was aware of the daily demands on my time and energy. He said he would be guided by me as to what I could cope with at home as regards Emma's health care which was now 24 hour care.

I thought back to the days when I first starting doing home IVs. I had thought then that the 2 weeks of home IV's was demanding but it was nothing compared to where we were now.

At first I started taking Emma home for weekends, Friday till Sunday. Her care consumed my every minute but it was good to have her home and difficult to leave her back to the hospital on the Sunday night. The plan was to gradually extend the weekends if all went well.

When Emma was in hospital during the week I would also take her out in the wheelchair with oxygen on board and we would go over to the nearby shopping centre for a short time just to give her a change of scenery from the hospital room. We discovered that going anywhere in the wheelchair took twice as long.

For Emma, I know there were times when it bothered her that she had to be in the wheelchair because she felt she was losing her independence. She didn't have the breath to walk so she had to be brought everywhere.

Sometime during the previous few months, I had prayed that God would tell me more about what Heaven was like. Emma's health was critical and if she were to die, streets lined with gold and pearly gates were not enough information for me about Heaven. I had so many questions and wanted detailed answer. How would she get to Heaven from this Earth? would she be lonely? (she was too young to have had anyone close to her who had died), would she be aware that Luke and I were not with her (She was not ready to leave us), what would it be like? I prayed for the answers to my questions. The answer to this prayer came in the form of a book that a friend of mine gave me.

The book was called '90 minutes in Heaven' and was written by an American man, Don Piper, who had been involved in a horrific car accident. He was pronounced dead at the scene of the accident and for the next 90 minutes he went to Heaven. At the end of that time he came back to life, it's an amazing story. In his book he describes what Heaven is like and it answered all my questions. He talks about how he got there in an instant and was not aware of the people he had left behind. He talks about the harmonious music he heard, the stunning colours he saw and about how he felt love like he had never felt before.

Sometimes at the worst moments of Emma's deteriorating illness I would imagine her in Heaven, healed, happy and no longer struggling with health issues.

In December 2005, I was starting the countdown of preparations for Christmas. It has always been my favourite time of the year and I wanted to celebrate it as best we could.

Emma was still coming home at weekends and in hospital during the week When she was home it was full time care with her two IV antibiotics three times a day, oxygen all day and night (portable oxygen if we went out anywhere), Bipap breathing machine to help her breathe through the night, overnight feeds for ten hours a night, Insulin, oral medicine (about 30 tablets a day), 6 nebulizers and all the other things that go with full time health care like keeping the equipment clean and washing the parts that need to be washed, liasing with the CF team, the oxygen company and the antibiotic delivery company. Although there was a lot of responsibility and 24 hour care when Emma was home, it other ways it gave the three of us the opportunity to settle into our home life again.

Luke had kept reasonably well but a course of oral antibiotics didn't clear an infection that he had. Dr. Greally thought it would be better for Luke to have a course of IV's rather than let it slide as if that happened he may have to be admitted over the Christmas period. So Luke was taken into hospital in the middle of December as this was an unplanned course of IV's.

There is always a great buzz in the hospital in December as the nurses and staff make a huge effort to have the place looking festive and to bring presents to the patients. Sometimes I would take Emma and Luke home for a few hours in the afternoon so they could be around their familiar surroundings of home and also to give them a delicious home cooked meal. Then I would bring them back to the hospital that evening in time for their night time dose of IV antibiotics.

On the evening of one of those days, I returned home from the hospital aching with exhaustion. Emma had wanted me to text her to let her know I got home safely. I was in my bedroom texting her when I caught sight of something out of the corner of my eye. Emma had left a present and card for me on my pillow. The card said…

"Here's a little something to say thank you for being you. You're the best. I know I said this present was for your Santa sock but I changed my mind and have thought of something else for your sock that you will like. I hope your dreams come true. You deserve it."

Lots of love
Emma x x x x

Even though Emma was going through so much she constantly thought of others. A couple of months earlier she had put together some shoeboxes for Operation Christmas Child which would be delivered to children in other countries who live in poor conditions.

Both Emma and Luke got out of hospital on 23rd December but before we left the three of us were given a Christmas present each. I was touched by the kindness of the hospital. I was glad to have Emma and Luke home and although Emma's routine needed round the clock nursing from me, it was better than the daily journey to the hospital and the endless hours spent trying to fill in time. We survived every bad moment together and tried to live every good moment to its fullest. Daily we lived with the uncertainty of not knowing what was around the next corner

13

Burnout

I think it's important to give a balanced viewpoint of our experiences with CF and to say that although Emma's health was full time care by now, Luke's health was reasonable. For the most part he kept well so long as he did his daily routine of oral medicine, physiotherapy and nebulizers. He had been on routine IV's twice a year for a fortnight each time but when we were going through Emma's health crisis his health was reasonable enough for him not to need his regular IV's. He kept active by going to the gym, youth club, football training and football matches for the club he belonged to. He was also keen to do football trials for the U16 of a premier league football club. I wanted to support him in this so I drove him the round trip of 50 miles two or three times to the training ground on the far side of the city. In this year when Emma's health was deteriorating, Luke coped admirably with all these stresses and got excellent results in his Junior Cert exams.

When I think of what we went through in 2006 I can still feel the energy drain out of me.

We had two routines. When she was in hospital I was spending up to 9 hours a day with her, adjusting to the slower pace of hospital life, spending time in her cubicle on the ward talking with each other, supporting Emma through the awfulness that she was going through, being there for meetings with Consultants, Nurse Specialists, the Dietician, Physiotherapists and others on the team, bringing Emma to different departments for tests like x-rays or blood tests, eating some of our meals together, enjoying the company of visitors, taking her off the ward down to the canteen or the hospital shop just so she had a change of scene, bringing her out in the wheelchair to the nearby shopping centre, talking with other parents of CF young people and generally being a part of hospital life.

Sometimes I was going back and forward to the hospital twice a day so I could also spend time with Luke at home particularly for dinner so he was not eating alone. I would try to set aside specific time one day of the week where Luke and I could have a couple of hours together either to have a meal together or to do food shopping (having food in the house is very important to a teenage boy). This weekly time meant we had some kind of quality time together. I wished I could have given him more time and attention but we were living in a constant state of crisis and Emma's health was priority.

I was very proud of the way he coped with the uncertainty of our daily routine. Many times I had to wake him up late at night or in the early hours of the morning to tell him I was taking Emma back to hospital.

Our other routine involved our life outside the hospital. Every time I walked out of the doors, life seemed to pick up speed. Daily, there was too much to do and time lost its meaning. I would have priorities to get through in a given day and would try to work my way through all of those before going to bed at night.

I was holding down a very part time job. Initially I had taken on the job in the card shop for 24 hours a week but when Emma's health deteriorated to 24 hour care I reduced my part time job to 10 hours a week.

There was also a certain amount of chores necessary to keep the household running smoothly. Things like cooking, cleaning, ironing and paying bills. I also tried to keep in touch with friends as much as possible.

When Emma was home I was giving her full time healthcare which included early mornings and late nights with the IV antibiotics administered. From 9.30pm every night until about midnight it was hours filled with nebulisers, oral medication, IV medicine (flush, first antibiotic over half an hour, flush, second antibiotic over half an hour, flush), setting up her Bipap machine, night time feeds and oxygen. It was part of daily life that she would be choked up with mucus. It would not be unusual in that time to have her leaning over the bathroom sink coughing up a murky colored mucus and crying because she just couldn't live her life like this anymore.

It was so heartbreaking, she didn't deserve any of this. I would gladly have switched places with her if I could. We stayed close to home as much as possible. We couldn't make plans for the future because we never knew when the next health crisis would happen. There were times when we seized normality in the form of a meal with family or friends, or going to the cinema, or some mundane everyday thing like household paperwork.

Dr. Greally, Dr. Basil and Ger, and the rest of the CF team at the hospital were very supportive and caring. They all contributed to providing us with excellent medical care.

We often stopped by the office of Margaret, the secretary, and she would make our appointments and chat to us. They were all fantastic, we couldn't have asked for a better team. The nurses, assistant matron, matron, art teacher, fund raising team, accounts personnel, kitchen staff and car park staff all became part of our everyday lives. All of them taking interest in our situation and offering encouraging and sympathetic comments.

Where I had a few hospital contact numbers in my mobile before, more had been added with each deterioration of Emma's health.

One of the good things was that Emma's health brought us closer and we had very good communication with each other. At times during the day when I wasn't at the hospital with Emma, we were in constant contact with each other by mobile phone. I always knew what was happening with her. At this stage our lives blended into one, everything revolved around Emma's health care and routine. For the most part Emma kept reasonably good humoured (considering what she was going through) and she was always thinking of others.

Many years prior to this we had been introduced to the Cystic Fibrosis Research Trust. It is run by a group of volunteers so there are no overheads. All the monies raised go directly to funding a Professor in his research studies for the year. One of the aims of the CFRT is to raise awareness of CF. They support research in Ireland as they believe that this helps patients in Ireland to receive the most up to date treatments. They run a yearly Shopping Spectacular to raise funds. We have supported this every year since Emma and Luke were toddlers. Many of our friends have also faithfully supported this.

In this time of critical illness, Emma was fundraising for CFRT so that hopefully some time in the future others with CF would not have to go through what she was going through. We had done small amounts to raise money over the years with

Emma making Christmas gift tags and me occasionally making matching handmade cards. Emma's latest idea was a calendar. This was printed and partly funded by family friends. It raised thousands for the cause that was so close to our hearts.

A nurse on the hospital ward, Ger C, who went the extra mile in her care for Emma had a cousin who offered to have his long hair shaved off and this raised thousands too.

This is what Emma remembers about her fundraising for CFRT…

I wanted to start fundraising for CF Research when I got really sick and spent most of the time in hospital. It took my mind off what I was going through. I could focus on something positive. I could use my artistic skills to help others instead of sitting watching television feeling sorry for myself and feeling terrible. I wanted to use my creative skills to make sure that a cure, or even a breakthrough, was found for CF so that other patients did not have to suffer like I was suffering.

People often commented that Emma looked so well, which was true she did look quite well…on the outside, but with CF the damage is inside the body, on the lungs, so it is only possible to see the true picture of the CF person's health on an x-ray or in the laboratory results of a cough swab that details the infections which are present and the level of these.

Our friends continued to be supportive with encouraging and affirming words. Simple things meant so much and lifted our spirits …a text message from someone to let us know they were thinking of us…a phone call to chat about how things were…a meal with a friend…a friend's husband used to come to our house and cut the grass for us…a cup of tea or lunch with a friend and a chance to sit down for a short while…friends would come to the hospital to spend time with me or Emma or both of us. I was constantly amazed by how many lives were being touched by what we were going through and was comforted knowing that we had the prayers of family, friends, our Church family, work colleagues, some of the teachers at Emma and Luke's school, and people in other countries.

I think it is important to say at this point that not everyone who is going for transplant is as unwell as Emma was. I wouldn't like to upset anyone if they thought that what we went through is possibly ahead for their loved one or themselves. Even Newcastle commented that they rarely see anyone with health as poorly as Emma's was. I have known of a young person on the transplant list who was still able to walk to the bus stop and another young man who drove himself to the hospital for his transplant operation.

Our experience was very different. This chapter is the longest chapter in the book and I think it has to be in order to get across the reality of what we were going through.

You know what it is like if you have a night of disturbed or broken sleep, multiply that tiredness by 372 consecutive nights and it will give some idea of part of what we were going through.

I had reached a point of physical burnout. My body ached with the daily demands on me. I had pains in my legs from stress. I often felt like I was going to collapse and that the doctors would not find anything physically wrong with me, they would just know that it was complete exhaustion. Complete rest and lots of sleep were what I needed but it was not even within the realms of possibility.

Think about a time when you were under extreme stress, now multiply it by 372 days. I had reached mental burnout. My concentration was poor and my memory seemed to be getting worse. I felt like I would lose my mind if we had to continue like this for much longer. In conversations, I would stumble over words. Sometimes I felt like my mind would explode if I had to take on board any more information. I was too tired to make decisions and yet there were so many important decisions to be made. There seemed to be so many forms to fill out for different things and I got to the point where, if we needed something and it involved filling in a form, I would put it to one side because I couldn't face filling it in.

Think about a time when a loved one was seriously ill, multiply your feelings about that time by 372 days. I had reached emotional burnout. I felt that I couldn't take any more heartache. I had never had anyone close to me die and now I had to face the fact the first death of a person close to me could be my beautiful teenage daughter. In the shop where I worked when I was serving a customer who was buying a sympathy card, I sometimes imagined what friends would say to us on the sympathy cards they would send to us if Emma died. The heartache of this brought tears to my eyes and I would have to blink away the tears. Sometimes I just felt numb but I think this was just my body's way of switching off to the awfulness.

Think about a time when you prayed about a serious situation that needed an immediate turn around which only God could orchestrate, multiply that intensity by 372 days of waiting. I am always reluctant to admit to reaching spiritual burnout. I feel that I am letting God down by doing this but at the same time I am so glad of His mercy and that He understands our times of stress and pressure. Although my faith in God remained firm and steady and I kept close to Him in prayer, in my exhaustion I often felt distant from Him or was not living my Christian life to its full potential. At times I was angry at life and frustrated with our situation. I knew God was the only one who had the answers to our situation, the only One who could help us through and I knew I didn't want to go through this without Him. I felt that beliefs I had held for years were being challenged. In these times of confusion I learnt more about the grace and faithfulness of God. I felt my relationship with God kept me safe in the eye of the storm we were living through.

I think the best way to describe the minute by minute rollercoaster of what we were going through is to share some of my diary entries which I wrote during that time. I didn't have the time or the energy to write a daily diary but sometimes I would write down my feelings to relieve the stress of the crisis we were living through. At the beginning of some of these entries there are sentences in brackets, these are not extracts from my diary, they are just a short explanation of something that happened that day or what we were going through at the time.

NOVEMBER 2005

(Emma spent 21 days of this month in hospital. I noticed as her illness progressed, she was not always able for visitors like she had been previously).
I have watched her go downhill in the past seven weeks since her Peg feeding tube operation. Part of me wants to pray that God will end her suffering and take her to Heaven to be with Him. The other half of me grieves for all the years that we would have to continue living here on this Earth without her, missing her smile, her winning personality, her mischievousness, her honesty and her mature analysis of life and circumstances. Cystic Fibrosis is robbing her of her quality of life. She has lived in the hospital for six of the last seven weeks. Her oxygen requirements increase all the time. Her temperature keeps

spiking. Her little feet were swollen and purple last week. Her overnight feed sometimes makes her sick.

She has been on IV's for four months. Her lungs are not working properly now and it's heart breaking sometimes to watch her trying to breathe when she is sleeping. The effort her body has to make just to breathe is awful.

When I was on the way to the hospital earlier today, Emma texted to say that if she did not see any improvements by the end of the week, she would give up. I asked her what she meant by giving up and she was not really sure but felt she could not live like this anymore. She had been given a nebuliser earlier but as soon as it was finished her oxygen levels dropped very quickly and she was now on about 7 litres of oxygen. She felt she may not make it through the day.

After these frightening text messages going back and forwards between us, I arrived at the hospital to see her wrapped up in a blanket, sitting on the bed, looking very sad and down. She barely uttered a word when I asked her how she was but soon she came around. I pulled up the blinds on the window and as she ate breakfast, we chatted and caught up on the news of what had happened to her. We switched on the TV and within a short time she was joining in the chat. Her mood was ok for the rest of the day... she even sat up and did a puzzle for a while and later I brought her down to the canteen in her wheelchair with oxygen....We heard later that after this morning's episode, Dr. Basil had left his phone number with the nurses so they could phone him if there was another emergency with Emma's health. Emma is now wearing a code blue monitor on her wrist.

On the way home in the car tonight Luke and I talked a bit about how bad things had become with Emma's health and then drove home the rest of the way in silence, each of us lost in our own thoughts.

People react in many different ways. Some people's eyes well up with tears when they hear how unwell Emma is. Others try to find the bright side. Others ignore it, leaving us in silence because they do not know what to say or they are trying to deal with their own grief or the grief of our situation. I think at times like this the best reactions are from those who continue to act as naturally as possible with us because in a time of crisis like this, we need some things to stay the same. So much else has changed.

JANUARY 2006

(I had started the divorce process in November 2004 and at the end of this month, January, I was to go to court about it. My Mum arranged time off work to help with minding Emma at home while I was at the court).

1st January, 2006

Two minutes to go till the New Year, so while I'm waiting I'll write down a few notes about today... I don't feel like I'm part of the team at work anymore. I feel like I'm missing out on my friendships with my colleagues and also my work as I am only there for a few hours each day. Sometimes I feel so tired I want to quit my job. There is a lot involved in Emma's overnight care from 9.30pm till midnight …If Emma sleeps through the night, I would hopefully have 6 hours sleep. Then it's time to finish the overnight feed, flush out the tube, give the next doses of IV's over an hour, give her oral medication before I go to work. You could say I've done a days work before I go to work and you would be right. When I come home from my two hours at work I should really go back to bed to catch up on sleep but I get busy doing nebulisers for Emma and Luke. After that is lunch and before I know it I'm into the afternoon and I just keep going. The lack of sleep catches up with me at 9pm when I'm exhausted and want to go to bed. I can't though because the night time regime is about to start all over again.

Today was awful. After work, organizing nebulisers and lunch we were about to go to the hospital appointment. The oxygen compressor was making it's usual hissing sounds when suddenly it went 'clunk'. We could hear the sound of the motor running but it wasn't making oxygen anymore. I phoned the oxygen company and they talked through what might have happened. When I was speaking to them on the phone the machine started working properly again. All of this delayed us getting to the hospital appointment and when we did get there everything seemed to go wrong...problems with finding a vein for a blood test...the registrars we had known for six months have moved on and we have to get to know the new ones now...news of a new treatment for Luke...stomach pains for Luke...the emotions of watching Emma struggle as she has to lie down for an x-ray but then having to sit up quickly to bring up more mucus...Emma understandably distressed when coughing up the horrible sticky mucus...the emotions of watching Emma being upset because she did not have enough breath to do her lung function test...hearing bad news of a test result for Emma ...It's all so awful.

I know people have different ways of coping with things. If I have my quiet time of prayer and bible notes in the morning and start the day with God then I feel the peace that He is with us whatever happens that day. On the days that I start without God, I struggle so much with anger, all we have to endure, fear of the future, the demands of her illness and anticipatory grief.

When it came to 9pm tonight I was exhausted... Yes you guessed it...the oxygen compressor stopped working again. I started up her overnight feeds after flushing her tube with water. Then I found the manual for the oxygen compressor and read it to try to find out what was wrong with it. I discovered that the filter needed to be cleaned. It should be washed and left to dry. As I didn't have time for this, I managed to clean the filter without water and when I put it back in the machine it worked fine. I started Em on her Bipap machine and went to prepare the IV's. I called into Luke's room to say goodnight and he was lying very flat in the bed as his stomach was still hurting. As soon as I could, I had a good cry because we just cannot go on like this.

9th January, 2006

I know it's 7.08am and I should be getting ready for work but I have to take a few moments to write down my feelings. I'm at the point of a physical and emotional breakdown. I cannot go on like this for much longer. The constant lack of sleep is killing me....As I write this my legs ache and my eyes feel so tired...I spent most of Friday crying but I know it's just exhaustion. I have to try to get some more sleep if I am going to survive this.

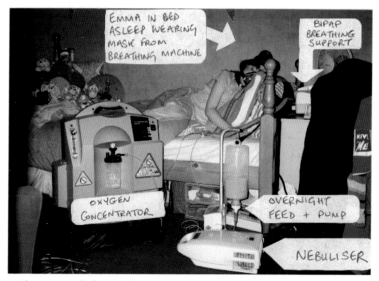

These were all the machines needed for Emma's overnight care when she was critically ill. She is lying in bed wearing the mask from the Bipap breathing machine. The tubing went from the end of the mask to the Bipap breathing machine on the unit beside her bed (to the right). The oxygen concentrator is the large machine in the centre left of the picture. In the centre right of the picture on the floor is her nebuliser and next to that is the over night feeding pump and feed.

Fridge full of medicine.

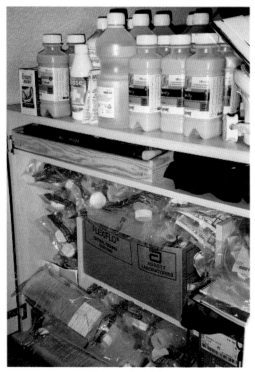

Overnight feeds.

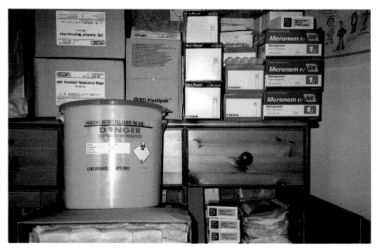

More medications.

FEBRUARY 2006

(I know there were times when I was not walking as closely with God as I wanted to. I always noticed straight away because my relationship with God would feel strained, I would feel like I had walked away from Him, I would have no peace in my prayer life. It was only when I would turn back to Him desiring to be more faithful in my walk with Him that I would feel His grace. Immediately my peace would return because I knew I was in a right relationship with Him again).

MARCH 2006

(When Emma is in hospital she is very much part of the hospital life. The nurses are becoming her friends. She knows what shifts they are working and they sometimes include her in their break times. She is known in so many departments. Often when I am wheeling her along the hospital corridors I feel like I have a famous person in the wheelchair because so many people wave, say hello to her or stop for a chat. The art teacher, Sarah, is great. She has such a bubbly character and is always very enthusiastic. She always tries to encourage Emma to do artwork and there are so many places within the hospital where Emma's artwork or poems are displayed on the wall).

APRIL 2006

(I don't always open my post on the day it arrives anymore. If I think it is something extra that will need to be dealt with, I leave it until another day when I feel

I can face it. Instead of an Easter Egg I gave Emma a present of a voucher for a local art centre where she can paint some pottery. We have tried to go there a few times but each time we have had to postpone it because she does not feel up to it or ends up back in hospital).

It's a year since Dr. Greally confirmed the deterioration in Emma's health and said that we had a window of opportunity in which to try to get her onto the transplant list. It's been a difficult year…When I think about the transplant… A major operation with six weeks recovery in England, then a new lifestyle learning how to detect daily if the body is rejecting the new lungs, plus a similar amount of daily drugs and a chance that some of those drugs could cause cancer or kidney problems.

I struggle with so much of our lives passing us by…waiting for improvements…waiting for change… It's not easy waiting when her health keeps deteriorating. I want to be the best Mum, carer, friend to Emma but I'm so exhausted that I feel I can't give my best because my resources are depleted. I want the nightmare to end.

5th April, 2006

(My divorce was finalized).

9th April, 2006

Special moments…We took Emma out of hospital to see Ice Age 2 at the cinema. The cinema is only a ten minute walk from the hospital. Emma was in the wheelchair and we brought portable oxygen with us.

17th April, 2006

I'm so tired and dizzy tonight. Emma was home for the weekend and we had some problems with the port in her arm not flushing (after the IV antibiotics have been given) on Saturday and Sunday night. I brought her back to hospital on Sunday after Church and typically the port flushed fine because it had had a rest on Sunday morning. Emma was tired when I brought her back to hospital tonight, she said her lungs ached. It's awful to see her suffering like this.

For some reason I kept wanting to look at photographs this weekend of Emma and Luke when they were younger. Some of the photographs were taken in 2003 which is not that long ago and Emma was quite well when those pictures were taken. Her health has deteriorated so rapidly in that relatively short space of time.

Sometimes I listen to her coughing up mucus, retching with the effort or I look at her when she is very ill and I think to myself that she deserves better than this, better than having poor health and not being able to live a normal life.

18th April, 2006

What do you do when you cry out of God for Emma's healing and nothing major happens...

It is so exhausting, work first and then today I had to try and do food shopping at the supermarket while Luke looked around for jeans and a shirt to wear for the Christening at the weekend...everything seemed to be taking so long and I felt under pressure to do things

quickly so that I could then get to Emma at the hospital.... It's getting more and more frustrating to not see a light at the end of the tunnel, to constantly be in a state of exhaustion, to never have enough time to do the things that need doing...
I don't know how much longer we can exist like this...How much longer until her healing comes?......I feel like screaming...we are continually living in a crisis situation, it's a nightmare.

21st April, 2006

...What kind of prayers does God answer anyway? I was going to say He is not answering the prayers for her healing but He is answering in a different way - not a physical healing but an emotional healing.
(I remember a friend passed an interesting comment a while back that it is a privilege to be given this level of suffering by God because it means He trusts me to be faithful. It was a profound thought that touched me deeply, challenged my thinking and changed my perspective. I came to the realisation that in every challenge I had faced there was a blessing of some kind if I persevered through and did not give up. Sometimes it was a lesson learnt, or an experience that when shared brought hope to others, or a characteristic change (more patience, calmer, less negative, stronger). So I learnt to look below the surface of life's difficulties to find a deeper reason and discover the blessing in it. It doesn't take away the awfulness, it just helps to make sense of it and find the purpose in it.)
Later Emma and I were texting each other about dreams and wishes. Emma texts "I wish there was a cure for CF

and not to have to have the transplant to lead a normal life".(Somewhere in the middle of all this madness and crisis, God gave Emma a verse of hope and comfort - Jeremiah 29 vs. 11. For I know the plans I have for you, plans to prosper you and not to harm you, plans to give you a hope and a future).

I know sometimes God speaks into a situation with a word of hope and often the reality seems far different from what He has promised. Then he changes things and brings them in line with His promises. (I was suffering burnout at this stage and could not take this verse on board but it brought hope to Emma and that's what she needed at this time. I'm so glad God completely understands us and is patient with us. I couldn't understand Him giving her this verse of hope when she was so critically ill. He knew I was reacting from a place of exhaustion and His verse of comfort to me was 'Be still and know that I am God').

22nd April, 2006

(My niece was being christened in Limerick this weekend. Emma was not well enough to travel so I stayed in Dublin with her. Luke went to the christening with family. It was a new experience that the three of us were not together for a family event like this. When I came home from the hospital after some mother/daughter quality time today , I was texting Emma and she said that she really enjoyed our time today. She thanked me for listening, helping her through everything, and for always being there for me when she needs me.

26th April, 2006

It breaks my heart to see Emma suffer so much. Tonight she was crying. She told me she's losing her self-worth because she can't do things for herself anymore - like walking up the stairs. She's finally given into the idea that we had been considering for a while, either we need a stairlift, or an extention out the back of the house so she can sleep downstairs. She's so tired this week, when I watch her struggle with the breathing I wonder how long she has left.

Will she make it as far as the transplant?...When she had shared her worries with me tonight about her deteriorating health, she had a good cry. I sniffed and she thought I was crying too. She said to me that when she cries I console her but she often wonders when I cry who consoles me? I didn't say it to her but the answer is no-one because I do my crying in private mostly.

28th April, 2006

… How much longer will this go on for? I can't bear to watch her suffer anymore, it's too much… She moans in her sleep and I keep thinking that she's having problems breathing but she says it's just because she is so tired…When she stops moaning I wonder has she stopped breathing. I was just thinking today that although it's constant care for her when she is home, it's great to have her home with us. I can't face going back to the hospital routine again.

3rd May, 2006

I'm amazed at what the human body and mind is capable of, how much it can withstand. Today my workload included...IVs starting at 6.30am, get ready for work, bring Luke to school, drive to work, two hours work, post a birthday present, home via the garage to pump up car tyres - 'air' not working, takeaway for Emma's lunch, clean out car for NCT car test, collect Luke from school, check air pressure on car tyres at another garage, bring Luke home, organise nebulizers for Emma and Luke, go to NCT car test, car failed, book it into garage for repair, arrange re-test, phone Dad, phoned school nurse, do Emma's IV's, bring Emma and Luke and a friend to their band practice, collect clock from jeweller friend, cut grass in front garden, make dinner, ironing for one hour, bath for Emma, wash and blowdry her hair, help her through panic attack because her breathing is bad today, do Emma's night time IV's, wash the filter in her oxygen machine, phone a friend, write a letter.

Now it's 1am and I have to be awake again for her next IV dose at 6am. Am so tired.

When I go in with the morning dose of IV's I'm afraid that one day she will have passed away in the night.

19th May, 2006

I feel like I have had an operation. You know that tender, sensitive feeling like it's going to be a while before you get back to normality. I just want to be protected and kept safe till I feel my strength return. All this has been brought on by the events of the last few days. Em and I had gone to Newcastle for her to have another assessment to see if she can go on the waiting list for a double lung transplant. Emma is very aware of her illness and all the complications so I think she was expecting them to say that these problems could be worked on and they would see us in another couple of months. I think she would have been happy with that. In many ways I would have been happy with that too. If they put her on the active transplant waiting list we have to have our bags packed and ready to go to Newcastle at a moment's notice if a set of lungs become available. I just want normality for us, I don't want to be away from Luke for 6-10 weeks. We have all had too much to bear already. Anyway they decided that she is sick enough to need to go on the transplant list and as well as she can be to survive it. She is to see the dentist who will check that she has no loose teeth before going on the transplant list and she also needs some vaccines. She is in the end stages of her illness, transplant is her only hope. (I know those words sound strong but it's the reality we were living with).

25th May 2006

(I'm looking at my Encouragement book for this month and I'm reminded of the postman with the Northern accent who delivered the post to the card shop I worked in. I don't know his name but he regularly stopped to ask how Emma was doing and was delighted to hear when she got onto the transplant list.
I'm also reminded of the day that Alan and Betty gave me a lift home from the garage because my car was in for repairs. Betty says I'm brave beyond measure. These are

just two of the encouragements in my book for that time. At the end of May, Emma's friends were finished Transition Year. Of all years for Emma to miss this one was not so bad as it would mean she would have less to catch up on. Though at the same time she had been so looking forward to the experiences of Transition Year and had planned where she would do her work experiences.

Her friends were maturing in some ways while she was maturing in wisdom through the life situations she was facing and so the gap was widening between them.

At the end of May we also knew that Emma would shortly be going on the Transplant List. We did not know if or when she would be called for transplant as it all depends on whether or not the lungs become available. During the waiting time we would have to keep within a certain radius of home because, if we were called, things would happen very fast to get her to Newcastle on time. In an effort of seizing the moment, we discussed going on a day trip to Belfast before Emma went on the transplant list. I had suggested this because we needed some time out and time together to make good memories which would always stay with us. Although as the day for the trip came nearer I was very nervous about taking Emma so far away from home while she was critically ill. I calmed myself with the thought that at any time we could turn back for home. Before we started out on the trip I gave her the morning dose of IV medicines, oral medicines and nebulizers. We brought her wheelchair, oxygen and more medicines with us. I got a few texts from friends when I was on the journey and I knew they were thinking of us and praying for us. We have mostly good memories of the day but there were times that I could see Emma was being very brave as it took a lot out of her to even do the basics like eating and breathing).

JUNE 2006

2nd June 2006

We had a stressful time earlier…We went to the local shopping centre before going to the hospital for Emma's appointment. I keep forgetting that it takes twice as long to shop when we have to bring the wheelchair, partly because we are confined to using lifts…We had so much trouble with the lifts…It was madness, absolute madness. We were supposed to be at the hospital at 2pm but we had to phone to say we would be later than that…Then we got stuck in a line of traffic. More stress. …We eventually got there almost an hour late.…Emma is very tired today, no energy. When we were home later I set about getting her meds for two nebulizers but when I looked into the front room she was sitting on the floor. I asked what was worrying her but she couldn't answer. I sat on the couch beside where she was sitting on the floor, she lay her weary head on my lap and cried. She said "I hate this life". All I could say was "I know". How could she not hate this life, even the basics like breathing are a struggle for her. As she cried, I prayed silently for her. A few minutes later she looked up at me with the look in her eyes and said "You've done it again". Whenever the children are upset, all it seems to take at times is a hug from me and they stop crying almost immediately.

4th June 2006

This afternoon we had a long tearful discussion about Heaven, what it's like, how can she be sure she will go there and what if it's not real. She had questions about faith and we talked about the peace that God gives us. I read to her from the book I had been given that described what Heaven is like. We cried together and let the descriptions of Heaven sink into our minds. The first time I read this book part of me felt that I wanted to go to Heaven then.

She sobbed in my arms as she told me that if she went to Heaven now she would miss me. My whole being aches at the thought of her not being here with us. I was able to reassure her that one day Luke and I would be with her in Heaven, nothing could separate us for eternity.

6th June, 2006

Well it's really 7th June 2006 as it's 1.19am. I'm just back from the hospital. I'm so tired, I should be trying to get some sleep but I have to write this down so I will remember how awful the tiredness and the situation is…It was a busy day again...

By 9pm I was beginning to wilt with tiredness. I just wanted to go to bed but instead I needed to stay up to do Emma's IV's. They should start at 10pm and if I got to bed by 11.30pm I would be doing well. I had hoped to take Emma out in the wheelchair to get some fresh air earlier but she said she would not be able for it as her breathing is not good today.

The weather is hot and humid and she is struggling to breathe. I was watering the plants in the garden when I heard her crying in the kitchen…She was distressed because she couldn't breathe…She is quite choked up with mucus today as well. I increased her oxygen level but it made no difference, so I got her nebulizer from upstairs and gave it to her. That made no difference either. She didn't want to go back to hospital and I don't want to have to go back to that routine either. She is only home from hospital two weeks and in that time we have also been back for her to see the dentist and to have vaccines in preparation for possibly being called for transplant.

I prayed for wisdom. Emma is due back in the hospital tomorrow for more vaccines but when she said she might not make it through it tomorrow, I decided it would be best to phone the Oak Ward. They had a bed available for her.

It's a cruel illness, she struggles so much to breathe. I was exhausted but I packed the bag for her, gave her the night time IV medicines and then headed for the hospital. The portable oxygen was not working properly and at one stage I had to stop the car at the side of the road, with her gasping to breathe and me trying to get the portable oxygen working.

We got to the hospital tired and stressed. Emma was struggling for breath. The nurses are brilliant, two of them were having their break at the front of the hospital, one of them took Emma's bags which we had at the back of the wheelchair and the other opened all the doors for us. I am beyond tired at this stage.

This is not quality of life for any of us. How much longer? How much more suffering for Emma? This is a nightmare. I am so tired, I can barely walk tonight, can't think straight, can't concentrate, my body aches, I just want to sleep.

7th June 2006

In the Bereavement Counseling home study course I am doing at the moment, part of today's lesson says there is a delicate balance between holding onto, letting go of and drawing close to the person who is dying. I'm finding this is true with Emma's health.

In my mind so many times I have let her go, released her into God's hands, asked Him to take her to Heaven so that her suffering on this Earth will end and she would be completely healed in Heaven. At the same time I want to hold on to her, I don't want to face years and years on this Earth without her, never hearing her infectious laugh, or having our heart to heart talks or sharing special moments. I don't want to let her go and be without this wonderful character and spirit. I would miss her too much. Most of all I want to draw close to her in her suffering so that she never feels alone, so she knows that I am with her even till the end of her life and that one day we will see each other in Heaven. Then there will be no more pain, sadness, dying or tears.

8th June, 2006

Emma has no energy to climb the stairs these days. She finds this difficult to cope with as she feels like she is losing her independence because of not being able to do basic things. So I created a fun way to help her up the stairs. She puts her arm around my shoulders and as I put my arm around her waist I lift her slightly. Her feet still touch the stairs but I am taking her weight to 'lift' her up the stairs. I call this the 'heavenly lift'.

Tonight Emma texted me from her bedroom to say "Hey Mum thanks for the heavenly lift..lots of luv Emma"

12th June 2006

(Emma's name has been placed on the transplant list. Sometimes the patient is asked to carry a 'bleep' but instead they have our telephone numbers).

16th June 2006.

I rarely ask "Why us?" I just get on with things and try to make the best of our situation. But today I'm falling apart. I'm beyond tiredness. I'm physically exhausted. I ache when I sit down, I can feel the tiredness hurt most in my legs and my eyes...I keep forgetting words, saying things that don't make sense...Since Emma went back into hospital I have been going back and forwards to the hospital twice a day because I come home to make Luke his dinner and spend some time with him... Today I drove 80 miles with school runs, hospital trips and work.

21st June 2006

2.47am! Longest day of the year. I woke to hear Emma moaning and crying. She had an episode earlier where she couldn't breathe so I increased the oxygen. This seemed to help for a while. I helped her up the stairs and she did her nebulizers early. She didn't go back downstairs as she wouldn't have the energy to get back up the stairs again. So we watched a DVD in her room.

Night time routine went as usual. I got to bed at midnight. Just after 3am she had more problems breathing so I increased the oxygen and gave her a nebuliser. I sat close to her…I could feel the bed thud with the effort of her breathing. (I prayed - O God, please take her to Heaven, she has suffered enough. Please take her in her sleep. I wouldn't want her to be frightened). Her breathing seemed to calm a little, there wasn't the same thud or effort, maybe her nebulizer is working. (I prayed again - O God, please give me the wisdom to know whether or not to bring her into hospital. I wish her suffering would end but I don't want her to die. I get a glimpse of the emptiness in our lives if Emma wasn't here and it makes me want to cry. Then I get a glimpse of Emma in Heaven, healed, happy, not struggling and I'm happy that she is smiling again not suffering). The neb seems to have worked, she talks to me, tells me that she feels so choked up by the mucus, says that they don't do much for her in the hospital. I think maybe she is in denial. The thing is they can't do much for her in the hospital anymore. She is dying a slow death. Daily deteriorating. She clings to hope and asks me 'Mum, if you hear something a few times does that mean it's for you?' Her friend has an article about salt treatment. Maybe it would help a little. It's such an awful disease at the end stages. She is so brave, she deserves better than this. I hug her, clean the filter on the oxygen compressor, start her Bipap and hope she can get some sleep.

27th June, 2006

(I did not always have the opportunity to cook a meal at

home so we ate at the hospital canteen, got takeaway or sometimes our local pub would plate up some carvery for us.

I noticed also that when Emma had been in hospital for a while and would be discharged, sometimes she would see a huge difference in our environment. There was lots of building going on at the time and often blocks of apartments would be built and Emma would have missed out on seeing them go up gradually.

Sometimes her text messages from her hospital bed were heartbreaking about how much she missed us and being home. I was in constant inner conflict because I wanted to be with Emma at the hospital all the time to support her through what she was going through but at the same time I had to divide my time between Luke and all my other responsibilities as well).

JULY 2006

(I did not know it at the time but two friends that I worked with often asked each other how could I deal with hearing things about Emma dying. They reckoned that the reality had not hit me yet. I suppose it's just a survival thing that a certain amount of emotions would have to be blocked out in order to survive the awfulness. It was a nightmare. My colleagues used to wonder how I could come to work and smile through the day with all we, as a family, were going through. I guess it was because work took my mind off things and I tried to enjoy the moment knowing that at any moment there would be more difficulties to face).

6th July, 2006

I think we are in for another bad night tonight. I can hear it in her breathing already. The weather is so warm and airless. Last night in the early hours of the morning I woke to hear a noise from Emma's room. I went to check it out and found that she was having breathing difficulties. It was 2.15am. As none of us are good at coping with broken sleep the next hour turned into a bit of a nightmare. Emma got into a panic attack and was distressed that her oxygen and Bipap didn't seem to be working properly. Although it was the same Bipap she had been using in hospital all week. I tried to phone the hospital. Then Emma let out a scream from her room. I ran to her room and saw fear and panic flashing across her eyes as she said, "This is it, I'm going to die". After trying one or two ways to resolve the crisis I decided Emma might be better off downstairs where it was cooler. I brought her Bipap downstairs to the front room. Then Luke sleepily stumbled out of his room to say he would help me bring the oxygen compressor downstairs. It was so heavy it took the two of us all our energy. We got everything sorted and I decided I would sleep downstairs with Emma in case she needed further help. She can't lie down to sleep as the chokes on the mucus so she was kneeling on the floor leaning up against a pillow on the couch.

I woke up just before 4am and felt cold so I got us some duvets and blankets. I fell into a deep exhausted sleep and woke at 7am when Luke came downstairs to get ready for a summer camp he was helping at… It's been a long day I hope for all our sakes she sleeps through this night. Alan (my brother) came over and fitted a ceiling fan in her room and that should help to keep the room cool for her.

9th July, 2006

While some are enjoying watching the World Cup finals and the tennis finals, our lack of normality continues…Emma's comment the other night about wanting to die in my arms shows me that she has thought through these things.

Today we were up early for the car boot sale. I did her IV's at 6am and Luke and I were in the queue by 7.20am. I kept in touch with Emma by mobile phone and if she needed me it would only take me 5-10 minutes to get home to her. She had debated about coming with us but I was glad she had decided not to because it would have been too much for her…it got very cold near lunchtime. When we got home I made lunch for her and did her afternoon IV's. Then Luke and I went to get some food at the shops. We also got takeaway and when we arrived home, Emma was feeling sick and breathless. She couldn't eat the takeaway and started panicking about her breathing. I phoned the hospital to let them know we were on the way there…she had another episode in the car where she was gasping and telling me she couldn't breathe. Then she would eyeball me with eyes of fear. She couldn't sit on the back seat of the car, she knelt on it gasping for air.

I phoned Rob from the oxygen company. He confirmed that we had the portable oxygen unit working properly and he also gave me advice on how to get more oxygen from the unit in an emergency situation…

When we got to the hospital her temperature and oxygen saturation were fine. They will continue her medicine as normal…Her health is such a nightmare and opens my mind to deep, serious questions which I had no answers to.

She has no quality of life. No energy, unable to eat, frightened with breathing difficulties, unable to walk up the stairs (crawls or I help her up), lost touch with teenage environment of school and socializing, can't have a holiday, can't enjoy a meal out or a film, her daily job is to breathe. Nightmare.

24th July, 2006

I think Emma must be on about her 19th week of IV's by now…I was so very tired that I fell asleep at the hospital today for two hours.

29th July 2006

(A friend would later comment to me, after reading a magazine article I had written, that she did not know the full extent of what we had been going through, she only got the surface of things. I suppose part of the reason for this is that I was coping with a lot of the difficult moments by myself in which I internalized my thoughts about what we were going through or wrote them down). It's so hard to settle to anything or to plan anything because we live in a state of crisis. I'm here writing a letter to a friend and in the middle of it Emma calls out to me for help. She has coughed up mucus inside the mask for her Bipap breathing machine. That has to be cleaned up immediately. When I get back to the letter writing, ten minutes later I have to stop because her IV dose needs to be finished.

30th July 2006.

I'm so glad to be home. I never want to go out again. Tonight we got free tickets to a fund raising event on the far side of the city. It was very interesting to see how the show was put together, the television cameras, the speed of the floor crew, the audience participation, the singers who were competing and listening to the judges comments. At one of the quieter moments we heard Emma's portable oxygen bleep...battery low. Normally we have 24 hours to replace the battery but for some reason tonight the battery just stopped working. She was getting no oxygen from the unit so we had an emergency on our hands.

Plan of action...get to the car as quick as possible, collapse Em's wheelchair and put it into the boot of the car, find a garage that sells 9V batteries., if we can't find one we have to get her home as quick as possible to get her other oxygen. It was all so stressful. There were delays getting to our car in the car park, sibling arguments, a car blocking me from following the flow in the car park and when we got to the garage they didn't sell batteries. We dropped Mum and Dad home and they had a 9V battery in their smoke alarm that we were able to use. It was all so exhausting.

As we drove home along the motorway, with the crisis over, Emma asked if I had enjoyed the evening. She had this amazing knack of bouncing back from a crisis so quickly but I was still suffering the after shock so my answer was twofold... Yes I had enjoyed the competition we were watching but not the emergency. One of the people who is part of our hospital family at this stage is Conor from the fundraising department. He is perfectly suited to this job as he is such a positive, energetic, people person. At the end of the fundraising event, we had given the flags and banners back to him but we couldn't stop to talk because of the emergency with Emma's portable oxygen. Conor later sent a text to my mobile phone to check that everything was ok with Emma. I thought that was very kind of him and was touched by his thoughtfulness.

AUGUST 2006

(When Emma's health had started to deteriorate a couple of years ago she bought an electric scooter. She wanted to have some independence in getting herself to places but did not have the breath to walk and could not travel by bus. Now as her health deteriorated further she began selling off things, feeling that she did not have long left to live. The scooter was one of the first things to be sold).

2nd August, 2006

It's so unfair that Emma has to put up with so much. She's just woken up and is now peuking up mucus. What a start to any day. I believe God is powerful and can sort out any situation but I struggle with why He allows the deterioration of her illness to go on for so long. Surely He could step in and give her total healing on this earth, or He could step in and say 'Enough is enough' and take her to Heaven. I know some day when I see Him in Heaven, I will know the answers but I want them now.

18th August, 2006

We can't live our lives like this anymore... This morning she is not breathing too well. She says her lungs hurt...She has a review at the hospital this morning and she does not want them to say she has to go back into hospital. So I explained that she can do her best to make sure that does not happen but after that it is out of her hands. She has already done her nebuliser and she is on oxygen. I've put her medicine downstairs waiting for her and the drink I put on the bedside locker will help her. Then I told her I was going to give her a hug because after that I need to sit down and rest...We were up at 6.30am to get ready to go to the hospital appointment at 8.30am. This is followed by a 9am hospital appointment and then her weekly review. Luke also has an Annual Assessment today. My legs are throbbing with the pain, all down the back of them, even sitting down and resting does not help. I can hear her crying again, I don't think this is going to be a good day.

(At the hospital her lungs were hurting but, amazingly, her lung function was up. She was allowed home with us but we were to bring her back if her condition worsens. She had a Glucose Tolerance Test today and she will be wearing a diabetic monitor for a few days to regularly monitor her blood sugar levels).

20th August, 2007

(4.30 in the early hours of this morning, I drove Emma back to the hospital. She had discomfort in her lower airways and couldn't breathe).

21st August, 2006

"I want to wear a wedding dress for a day" Emma said to me as her eyes sparkled brightly. Partly because she had seen the idea on one of her favourite programmes where the girls sit around in wedding dresses and watch DVD's. She also admitted it was because she would probably not live long enough to ever get married. It breaks my heart when those kind of realizations strike home to her. It's hard enough for her to face all she has to go through without her dreams crumbling in front of her eyes as well. She is so brave, so strong in her mind. She is amazing and deserves so much happiness and love.

23rd August, 2007

In a crisis situation, time sometimes loses meaning. There are so many things to be done so I tended not to think of 'What time is it?' but rather 'What's next?' and so that's how I found myself to be awake at 1.30 in the early hours of the morning making a Mummy costume for Luke to wear at the club he was helping at the next day. I got some of his old clothes and stitched on strips of white sheet so he would look like a Mummy when he was wearing them. I couldn't be at the club the next day to put the white strips of bandage over his face to complete the costume but a friend gladly helped out.

2nd September, 2006

This morning I sat in bed and wrote the format for Emma's funeral service or Thanksgiving service for her life. I think it's a combination of things that brought me to this point. When I look back over the last year she has spent most of it in hospital…The most we got her home for was 3 weeks, the least was 24 hours. Between September and December so many times I thought she was going to die but she bounced back. This road seems so long. It's so unfair that she has to suffer like this. She has a wonderful bright personality which brings so much love into people's lives…It's awful to hear her voice realities and conclusions she has come to, like "I'm not going to live long". This week I'm exhausted as I have a strep throat which is draining me of energy…I know she's on the transplant list but somehow it never seems like it will ever be a reality. As I write the order of service my eyes well up with tears and my heart aches at the sadness and grief that is before us. I chose songs like, 'My Jesus, My Saviour' because that's a favourite of ours. We have often chosen it for special occasions like Baptisms and Confirmations. I also chose the 'Blessed by your Name' song because some of the lines in it have been going through my mind recently as I have absorbed the truth of them. Some of these words are…

You give and take away,
You give and take away,
My heart will choose to say
Lord blessed be Your Name.

To me, this meant that if God said it was best for her to have her healing in Heaven, we would have to accept that in His wisdom He had done the right thing and we would still have to choose to bless His Name.

The other song I chose was 'Because of You', which talks about Heaven...

'There's a place where the streets shine with the glory of your Name, there a place we can go there we can live there beyond time'.

The words continue to talk about how there will be no more pain, dying or suffering in Heaven.

For her Thanksgiving Service I had two other special ideas. One was that we would play the 'You raise me up' song which had become so special to us during the past few months of her illness. As this song was played we would show happy photographs on the Powerpoint of Emma laughing and smiling. After the service we would give the children bubbles to blow outside the Church and as they blew them we would think of how free Emma was in Heaven, healed and happy, after being so cheated of breath when she was on this Earth. I had even written the announcement for the newspaper that would tell how Emma had been an inspiration to all for the way she coped with her long term illness. How her smile lit up the lives of those who knew her. How she was deeply loved and missed by us all, family, friends, and a wide circle of friends. (I can't believe that a year later as I write this book there is so much pain still inside from that time. The tears are dripping off my face. I feel like I'm going to choke with the pain in my throat. I can barely see the screen because my tears have fogged up my eyesight. In a way it's been healing for us to write the book).

(I had started to write a list of what I wanted to do if I had more spare time. I knew if Emma died there would be huge void in my life and initially I would not feel like doing anything. I thought the things on the list might help to keep my time occupied and gradually I would find a way out of the time of grief).

5th September, 2006

Emma is coming home from hospital today. This would be a typical example of the routine for that day.

7am	Alarm goes off, hit snooze button. Emma texting from hospital. She is on her morning dose of IV's and texting before she goes back for her lie-in.
7.10am	Out of bed and shower.
7.30am	Dry hair, get ready for work.
7.50am	Bring Luke to school then I go on to work for 2 hours. Eat nuts and yogurt in car for breakfast.
9am-11am	Work in card shop.
11.15-1.15pm	Shop for food messages. Eat packet of crisps in car. Not hungry enough for proper lunch.

1.15-1.50pm	Collect Luke from school and drop him to the gym.
1.50-2.10pm	Home. Phone Emma.
2.10-2.35pm	Put away food messages.
2.35-3.15pm	Empty car after car boot sale four days ago. Didn't have the energy to clean out car then. Put things up into the attic.
3.15-3.25pm	Quick shower and change.
3.25-3.35pm	Quiet time, interrupted by mobile. I'm needed as chauffer for the gym run.
3.35-3.50pm	Collect Luke from gym.
3.50-3.55pm	Write anniversary card for friend.
3.55-6.30pm	Travel 5 miles to hospital. 2 trips to the car park. First trip with Em's stuff. Lifts at car park broken, security man waited with the wheelchair while I drove down to the disabled spot at level one. Back to the ward to collect Emma. Said our goodbyes to the nurses. They gave me the usual list of her medicines detailing the eight times a day that she needs her doses…6am, 10am, 12 noon, 2pm, 6pm, 8pm, 10pm and midnight including her IVs 3 times daily, Drove 5 miles back home. Delivery man waiting

at our door with Emma's medicine delivery.

6.30-7.10pm   Put medicine in fridge. Keep out tonight's dose. Put clothes on line to dry. Make dinner. Phone hospital about dose of medicine for afternoon meds tomorrow.

7.10-7.35pm   Sit down and eat dinner. Great to hear laughter in the house again and to have a home cooked meal together.

7.35-7.55pm   Talk with Emma and Luke.

7.55-9.35pm   Church prayer meeting 5 mins away. Have mobile with me in case I have to be contacted urgently.

9.35-10pm   Home. Chat with Emma and Luke. Arrange work experience with my brother Alan as part of Luke's transition year in school.

10.00pm   Emma's IV's medicine routine starts and as I am waiting for the first dose to go through I iron some clothes. It may sound strange but I am delighted to do this normal piece of housework as it has been piling up for the last two weeks and all I have had the energy to do is look at it.

11pm	Emma is asleep. Flush her line and begin her second IV.
11.30pm	IV finished. Flush her line.
11.40pm	Finish watching TV programme. Lights out.

(This week before Emma had been discharged from hospital, she was put on an extra IV. The two she was already on which were injected into her three times a day were not maintaining her, she was slipping away. She had reservations about going on the 3rd IV because she felt that if this was added to her treatment she would never come off it).

This is what Emma remembers about the situation:

Well, were do I start. When I was told I had to have a tube inserted in my stomach (PEG) I just thought you got to be kidding. It wasn't that long since I had to answer the biggest question of my life, to chose to have a double lung transplant or not.
The first attempt to get the tube in ran into problems and I ended up on a ventilator for two hours which I don't remember. When I woke up I heard someone say " we couldn't go ahead with the procedure". Then I felt my stomach and there was nothing there. I was not impressed at all. I thought this meant I would not be assessed by Newcastle but I was wrong. It just meant they would have to try again soon to get the PEG in. Even though I was told I could opt out of the process leading up to transplant at anytime I wanted to try my best to strive to live. The

second attempt of this operation would be done in another hospital. The second time it was successful. The PEG tube was in and I could start getting the feed and helped to put on weight...the thing that was most frustrating was... I started to get reflux. If that wasn't enough I developed diabetes too. At this stage, I was numb from hearing bad news one after another after another. I just started to accept all the hits. It became normal to me. It was like I was nearly expecting bad news and if I got good news I was just waiting for the bad news to come next. Knowing that my health was so bad was hard at first. It was frustrating beyond words. I remember crying out to God asking questions till I was blue in the face. " Why?" "I'm only 14 why am I dying?" " I should be having fun in 4th year. Fighting with my Mum cause I came home at 2am on a school night. Choosing what I want to experience... Choosing what club to go to at the weekend. Instead I'm sitting on my death bed in hospital wondering if I'll make it through the next day... You say, "Where two or three are gathered in my name there I am in the midst of them." I know there is an army of people praying for me. I'm not getting better. In fact I'm deteriorating every day; every minute. You said you love me so much you sent your son, one and only son, to die on the cross for me. How can you say that? I'm dying at 14.

Sometimes I cried so much I ended up having a coughing fit. I'd cough and bring up a lot of mucus. This was an indescribable horrible torture. I'd cough endlessly. I always knew if I'd be there for a while. It was like I just couldn't stop. I'd be bent over the sink throwing up a murky colored mucus. Sometimes I wouldn't even get to the sink cause I'd be coughing so violently. It was exhausting. The horrific thing was that even the times I felt like I was dry of muscus and couldn't possibly have any more I knew there was always more, lots more...It was so draining. At times when the coughing really got to me I'd start to cry which didn't help but I couldn't stop cause I was upset about my situation. Then I got frustrated that I couldn't breathe cause I was coughing and crying and couldn't stop...Things were not going to change. I just had to make the best of the situation I was dealt. Not being able to breathe just became the norm for me.

One day I was talking to Mum asking lots of questions and crying again. That day Mum convinced me to stop focusing on what I was going through, and to try and distract myself with things I like to do. I decided to help raise funds for CF research so people wouldn't have to suffer like I did. I did as much as I could no matter how small it was, like a raffle. I learnt to deal with my weak body. I knew my limits. I did my best to make the best of my situation living in the moment. From time to time I still reflected on what could happen but not to the same extent as I had before. I still cried from time to time but I had no more energy to become frustrated. I guess I just accepted the reality but still had hope I'd live. My relationship with God at this point was up and down. One minute I'd be frustrated at Him, shouting, screaming and doubting Him, His love and His existence. The next few minutes or hours I'd be back apologizing to Him. This could go on for several times in a day sometimes. During this time I felt God was quiet with me. They say it is in the silence that you can hear God the loudest. You just have to be patient and willing to hear Him whatever He has to say no matter how hard. When I got to that point God spoke to me. I was in church one day. I heard this verse Jeremiah 29: 11 " For I know the plans I have for you, declares the Lord, plans to prosper you not to harm you, plans to give you a hope and a future". It just hit me. Twice I asked God to confirm the verse to me and He did. I clung to it. I was still getting worse even though I was proclaiming that verse.

When I asked God, "Am I going to die?" or in any way made reference to me dying it didn't feel right inside. It's hard to explain. It was like God was telling me that's not going to happen. Like He was saying " It's ok everything will be fine. Trust me."

I really struggled with my faith. I knew I had to stay close to God though. He knew the way. I had to totally surrender so He could fully take over. I had no power over what was happening to me neither did the doctors, nurses, friends or family. What I couldn't see He could. I just had to trust Him and totally surrender to his will. Life or death. It's easier said than done. I used to pray to God "OK. Fine. I surrender. Whatever Lord. WHATEVER. Life or death. Just stop this suffering. Enough is enough. Let Your Name be glorified just do it now. Please." Then a while later I'd realise what I'd said and come back to Him and ask Him to forget what I had said… Eventually, I got to the point that I surrendered. I was so weak I just didn't care what happened. I got to the point I had no energy to pray or spend time with God. I couldn't concentrate. God also comforted me and gave me peace with the words of a song called "You Raise me up". I knew I couldn't do this with my own human strength but I could with God's strength.

This is what Luke remembers about the 372 days that Emma was critically ill:

The year that Emma was 24 hour care and was in a critical condition I felt really bad for her because she was missing out on normal things that people her age were doing. She was slowly getting worse each day so the most she got home for was a few weeks.

I was in third year at school and doing my Junior Certificate... I was getting worried about Emma cause she spent most of her time in and out of hospital that whole year. I also didn't know if I was going to go down the same road or what was going to happen to me within the next year or two. It was very worrying to see my sister suddenly go down hill rapidly and not knowing what the future had in store for our family. She would only get out of hospital for a few days at a time and then would have to go back in, which shows how ill she was. It was a big shock when my Mum told me that Emma had to go onto the transplant list, even though her health was bad I didn't think that it would come to that. I just wanted her pain to be over and that she would get new lungs soon. Mum would try and spend time with both Emma and I. As I didn't always like going into the hospital because all I could do was sit around, I would stay home some of the days. When I got home from school, I had a lot of time at home by myself. It was ok I did home work, had some food, did some physiotherapy and some days went out to play some football. It was weird at the start not having Emma at home or Mum here as much but then you just get used to the situation.

I remember that sometimes Emma would just suddenly not be able to breath and Mum would have to rush Emma to hospital in the middle of the night. Each time Mum would cope brilliantly and calmly. For that whole year our whole life just revolved around the hospital. Some of the days I went into school then home quickly and straight to Emma.

We would be eating in the car a lot cause we never had the time to stop. I still kept up the usual football and all of my activities. For Sunday dinner we would sometimes go to our local pub and they would put the carvery onto plates so we could bring it to the hospital.

Our family and friends came to visit Emma which would break up the day..

I don't think too deeply about bad situations and that is how I deal with them. I just cope with the practicalities of the situation. When the bad situation is finished I don't think back over what happened I just move on.

14

Wedding Dresses and Drama

On 6th September, the day before Emma's 17th birthday, I drove into Dublin's city centre with her to look for a wedding dress. She wanted to act out the scene from one of her favourite TV programmes where the girls sit around in wedding dresses and watch DVD's. She had also mentioned to me a few weeks before this that she thought she may not live long enough for her ever to have her own wedding.

We had heard of a shop where they sold secondhand wedding dresses for an incredibly low price which suited both our budget and also the fact that Emma was just going to use it for a few hours. I parked the car and walked over to the shop with Emma in the wheelchair. Unfortunately the wedding department was upstairs. Emma climbed slowly up the stairs with her portable oxygen tank on her back. When she reached the top of the stairs she needed to rest on the couch. I collapsed the wheelchair and carried it up the stairs. Emma had a very definite design in mind and nothing there matched it. So after browsing for a while, we went home with no dress.

The next day, 7th September, was her birthday. We had planned to have the family and some friends over for an open house. Emma would not have the energy for a party but an open house where people came and went at different times would be manageable for her. We planned snacks, cocktail sausages, pizza and her favourite birthday cake with her name iced on top of it. I was in work for two hours that morning, having done her IV's and medicines for an hour beforehand. On the way home I stopped at the shops to buy the party food and a present for Emma from Luke. When I was queuing to pay for the food I got a text message from Emma to say she was having trouble breathing and she needed my help. I rushed home immediately and tried increasing the oxygen, giving her nebulizers and medicines to help her. Her breathing calmed a little. I felt we should cancel the open house but she pleaded with me not to. I explained to her that she would not enjoy having people there because her breathing was so bad and she could not walk more than a few steps without having to cough up lots of mucus. It was heartbreaking.

She had nothing to look forward to if the open day was cancelled. All she would be doing for the whole day was trying to breathe, trying to survive. She had only been discharged from hospital two days before this. I contacted them to let them know how she was struggling with her breathing. The team were sensitive to the fact that she would not want to go back to hospital on her birthday but reassured me that if I needed to bring her back in that was ok with them. Reluctantly we cancelled the open house but when her breathing calmed a little over the next couple of hours she wanted me to text everyone again to tell them the open house was back on. Her body was weak and fragile as she was in the end stages of her illness, we would find out later that by now she only had a month left to live. However the positive qualities of her personality were still very much intact. She had always had lots of determination and a great attitude towards living life to the full. She rarely let her illness get her down. Now that her breathing had improved a little she wanted to seize the moment and celebrate her birthday with the family. It turned out that her breathing relief was only temporary, if she moved a few steps from one place to another she would be gasping for air. She had multiple infections on her lungs at this stage of her illness. She had no appetite today because of the effort it was taking to breathe and also the taste of the infections in her mouth. At one point during the afternoon, she cried in my arms as she said "I can't live like this anymore". My heart ached for her, this was no way to live. I wished I could make things better for her.

Our friends, Fern and Sarah (mother and daughter), called by with a birthday present for Emma. What I only found out months later was that when they left our house that day and were back in their car, they admitted to each other that they thought Emma did not have much longer to live. They cried together at the thought of this.

A friend from work had sent home a wedding dress and tiara for Emma to wear while she watched a DVD. So we dressed Emma up in the dress, took some photographs and watched a DVD. When the film was over, Emma said she wanted to get back into her regular clothes. She was exhausted at this stage and found the weight of the dress too heavy.

Shortly Luke arrived home from school, our neighbour and friend had given him a lift. We spent a quiet afternoon together. Emma wasn't able for much more than sitting watching television. Luke did his homework and afternoon nebuliser. I kept busy doing housework, the medication regime and monitoring how Emma was doing in case I needed to rush her back to hospital. In the late afternoon, Luke set up the Playstation for himself and Emma. We had all coped with the deterioration of Emma's health in different ways over the past year and I had noticed that one of the ways Luke coped was to take on the role of trying to keep us cheerful and lightening the mood for us whenever he could. I appreciated this afternoon when he set up the Playstation for them both as it would keep Emma's mind off her difficult breathing for a while.

Later in the day I had started making dinner when the telephone rang. Someone at the other end of the line said "This is Newcastle, we think we have a set of lungs for Emma".

The only way I can explain the impact of that phone call is to say that I felt we had been living in a war zone, exhausted by the daily crisis and trauma of Emma dying and all of life's challenges, to hear these words was like hearing the helicopters coming into that war zone to lift us out of the horror we had been living through. I knew there was the potential that these lungs would not suitable but I never for one moment considered this. This call had been so unlikely. Emma was the size of a twelve year old and they had not had that size in the previous twelve months. Her health was so fragile and there was so much going against her, now hope of a positive outcome flooded through me. I had a peace inside me that this was her chance, everything was going to be okay now. I put my hand over the end of the telephone and had a silent cry to myself while Kirsty, the transplant co-ordinator, spoke to me. At one point she commented that I had gone very quiet. Choking back the tears, I told her that I never thought this call would come.

When the phone call finished I was in shock I couldn't remember whether Kirsty had said that I was to call the ambulance, or she would call the ambulance or it would just arrive at our front door. Something was happening in half an hour and we had to be ready.

I went back into the room where Emma and Luke were

playing Playstation. I said to them "You will never believe who that was". When I told them it was Newcastle, Luke sat frozen with the Playstation controls in his hands. Emma leapt to the far side of the couch she was sitting on and in a panicked voice told me she thought she was not strong enough to go through a transplant experience.

I have never had such a huge sense of God going before us. It was like as if He had every step planned and we just had to step into the moment. It was incredible. I even felt that He gave me the words to say because at the point that Emma said she couldn't go through it, I opened my mouth and words of wisdom came out. I said to her that if someone had told her at the beginning of this year what health issues she would go through, she would have said she could not do it. However, she had come through it step by step and would come through the transplant experience the same way. I was able to say to her that even before we knew she would be called, God knew and had been preparing her. Her poor appetite that day meant that she was fasting for an operation she had not known she would be called for. The fact that the open house was cancelled meant that she had had a more restful afternoon and was not overtired for this major operation. It also meant that she would have a less upsetting send off. Although it would be great to be surrounded by the love of family, it would be very emotional.

I was aware we only had half an hour and time was ticking away. My mind went into overdrive as I made a mental list of the necessary things that had to be done at short notice. First priority on my mind was that I had to sort out Luke's routine and accommodation. My next priority was to let family and friends know what was happening. I made four phone calls. I phoned Alan, our Minister and friend. He knew how ill Emma was and when he heard my emotional voice he thought I was phoning to tell him that Emma had died. He was going to the prayer meeting that night at Church and he would let others know so they could pray for us. I also found out later that he kept a vigil through the night. He said I could contact him anytime to let him know how things were progressing with Emma. It was such a comfort to have this support and encouragement.

I then phoned my Mum to ask her to tell the rest of the family. I would keep in touch by text and then she would forward these texts to the family to keep them up to date. School had just started again after the summer holidays and I felt it was important for Luke not to miss out on his schooling. We did not know how long Emma and I would be in Newcastle, it could be up to ten weeks between her operation and the recovery time. My Dad's health was not good at this time and my brothers and sister did not live near us, so I felt that it would be better if Luke stayed locally. In that way he would be able to keep his routine which I think is important at a time of crisis because it gives the reassurance that while some things seem out of control, others are remaining the same.

My friends, Bruce and Fern, who had minded Luke previously when Emma and I had traveled to Newcastle for assessments had very kindly said that if Emma was ever called for transplant, Luke was welcome to stay with them. I phoned Fern to let her know about Emma's call for transplant and she arranged to collect Luke shortly. He just needed some time to pack a bag and get his medicines together. When she heard about the turn of events she, too, realized how significant it was that the open house had been cancelled.

I phoned Emma's year leader from her school who had very kindly offered to help out with school lifts for Luke anytime. He lived nearby and would be able to arrange to collect Luke for school and bring him home every day. I really appreciated this and was thankful to have all this support during our crisis.

I had half an hour to pack. When Emma had been placed on

the active transplant waiting list we had been told to have our bags packed but if we had packed in the Summer and got called in the Winter we would have not had enough warm clothes with us. So I had not packed at all. Also we had to bring a 24 hour supply of her medicines and nebulizers with us because if the lungs were not suitable we would be sent home the next day. This meant that packing these would be a last minute thing as we were using them everyday. I was amazed at how I got everything packed in half an hour and ever since then it has changed the way I pack if I am going away anywhere.

I noticed that Emma had gone upstairs to her room and was very quiet. I met her coming down the stairs and asked if she was ok. She looked at me and said "This may be the last time I see you". Although it was breaking my heart that she could die in the operation I knew the transplant was her only hope at this stage. There again, I opened my mouth and the words just tumbled out. I said to her "You will never not see me again because you and me and Luke are spending eternity together. So even if you die in the operation (and you won't because this is your chance) you will see me and Luke again. For you it will be like the twinkling of an eye". It had to be God given strength that helped me to reassure her with those words because later when I thought about it my heart ached at the thought that she might die in the operation. For her it would be like the twinkling of an eye before she saw us again in Heaven but for us the reality would be many, many years of life here on earth without her. At that moment everything was a panic and all I could do was hug her and promise her I would talk more in the ambulance or the plane when things were calmer.

I noticed in the previous months when I was ready for things they just happened naturally. Sure enough as soon as our preparations were ready the ambulance arrived and they put our bags and medicine into it. Emma was disconnected from the oxygen tube which led from her, all the way up the stairs and onto the oxygen compressor in her bedroom. She was then connected to the oxygen supply in the ambulance. I found the calmness and helpfulness of the ambulance men reassuring. When one of them saw that I had everything ready and was organized, he passed the comment that we must have done this before. With all that had happened to us over the previous year we had become used to dealing with the trauma and crisis that comes with 24 hour care.

Neighbours and friends gathered to wish us well. I had said goodbye to Luke inside the house as I was sure that being a teenage boy he would not want his mother getting all emotional on the driveway in front of everyone else. I didn't want Luke to have memories of his mother and sister being taken away in an ambulance but there again I believe God was one step ahead of us. Three young boys whom I had minded in after-school care during previous years were standing with Luke on the driveway. When we left they went into the house and talked about normal stuff with him. He told me later this had helped as it meant he didn't have time to think about Emma going off for transplant.

When Emma and I were in the ambulance, I heard this deafening roar of engines. It turned out to be the noise of the motorcycles from the Garda escort that would get us through the motorway traffic to Dublin Airport. They 'leapfrogged' the ambulance and got us to Dublin Airport in 20 minutes. It was all very action packed. If the circumstances had been different Emma may have enjoyed the drama of it all but as it was she had gone understandably quiet on the journey.

We waited in the ambulance on the runway for the charter plane to arrive to take us to Newcastle. When the Sergeant heard that it was Emma's 17th birthday, he tried to keep the mood light by telling her he would set her up on a dinner date with one of the Garda.

I can still picture the evening. At the start of our flight we had a beautiful red sky and calm conditions for flying. Part way through the journey I noticed the full moon in the night sky glistening over the water. Everything seemed so calm and yet we were in the middle of an emergency which could give Emma a second chance at life.

True to my promise I tried to talk to Emma about the questions she had had earlier. However she started to feel weak and so I ended the conversation as I did not want to upset her. We were both so exhausted we slept for a while.

We arrived in Newcastle at a quiet time of the night which meant the journey by ambulance from the runway at Newcastle Airport to the hospital was not hampered by traffic.

The corridors of the hospital were equally quiet and soon we were settled on Ward 27.

The next few hours passed in a series of tests and talks with the transplant co-ordinator and the doctor. Sometimes people are called for transplant but the lungs turn out not to be suitable. They have to go home and wait again. The doctor reminded us of this but I had this feeling in my spirit that they would be. This was Emma's only chance. If she was sent home she would surely die. We waited for an hour to hear more about the lungs. Emma always had deep questions about things, so while we were waiting, she asked me how would I live without her if she died. I said although it would be devastating because I would miss her so much, I knew that one day I would see her again in Heaven. That thought would keep me going in the tough days of grief that we would have to face. (Even now, a couple of years later, the thought of how close we came to losing her has tears streaming down my face). Typical of Emma when she was facing a major health crisis she was thinking of others and she let me know that she was worried that if she died on the operating table I would have to face the journey home alone. They were heartbreaking discussions to be having but I did not dwell to much on these issues as I concentrated on the feeling in my spirit that things were going to be OK.

When Kirsty and Dr. Gerry came to tell Emma that the lungs were suitable, they asked Emma if she wanted to go ahead with the operation. It had to be her decision as, at 17 years of age, she was treated as a young adult and also she would be the one who would have to put the effort into recovery and aftercare to get the best use of the new lungs. I was so afraid for her that she would say she needed more time to think about it. Time was not on her side. In true Emma style of thinking things through and wanting her questions answered, she asked what were their statistics of patients dying on the operating table. When her questions about risks of surgery were answered, she looked at me and said "I could die on the operating table" and I had to say to her lovingly and in her best interests "If you don't go ahead with it you could die anyway, this is your only chance".

Dr. Gerry has often remarked since then about how strong it was for me to be able to say that at that time and he asked if I am a spiritual person. I am, my faith in God has always given me strength and hope particularly in the difficulties I have faced. At the time I said that to Emma I was just thinking of her. I knew she was frightened of this operation, (who wouldn't be?) but I also knew that if she said no to these lungs she would not survive to get a second chance because her time was running out fast. She was trusting me to give her the best advice and I didn't have time to sugar coat it. I knew she was looking to me for an honest answer. She had been whisked away from everything familiar, all the doctors and nurses she had learned to trust in Dublin. Now she had to trust a new set of doctors and nurses for the most important operation she would ever have in her life.

She told the co-ordinator that she would go ahead with the transplant.

Finally at 3am the moment came for Emma to go to theatre. I walked behind the trolley that she was sitting on. She was so brave sitting upright facing into the operation ahead of her. When she got to the pretheatre room, Emma asked questions about everything they were doing to prepare her for the operation. The anaesthetic seemed to take longer than any other time and she looked like she was going asleep in slow motion. I was so exhausted so when she was asleep I choked back the tears and went back to ward 27.

The nurse had said that I could go back to the cubicle that Emma had been in and have a rest. I was shattered, I had been awake since 6am in the morning, that's almost 21 hours and most of them were crisis care. Emma would be in theatre for about 5 hours so I told myself that I could sleep until 8am when Emma needed me again. I fell into a deep exhausted sleep knowing that Emma was in the best hands, family and friends were praying for us and God was watching over us. Apparently the nurses checked on me from time to time to give progress reports on Emma but I was out cold.

Dr. Gerry, was so wise, he told the nurses this was probably the first decent sleep I had had in a very long time. He was right. I woke up at 8am and shortly a nurse came to tell me the old lungs were out and the new ones were just about to be put in. She gave me a key and swipe card for my accommodation in the flats at the back of the hospital grounds. A while later it was apparent that Emma would not be out of theatre for a while so I decided to go the restaurant for something to eat.

Another thing I noticed about our time in Newcastle was that if I thought about someone shortly afterwards I met them. I had just been thinking about some questions I would like to ask Dr. Gerry when I met him as I was going into the lift. It was great to have a chat because he was able to fill me in on some of the things that were ahead for Emma in recovery. He put into words what I had known in my heart anyway, if Emma hadn't got the lungs now it would have been too late in the not too distant future. From the state of the old lungs when they took them out, they knew she would probably only have lived a month. The combination of IV antibiotics she was on was also an indication of how bad things were. He asked how Luke is with his CF and he acknowledged that my situation is very different. He said that they were very impressed with Emma's strength but even more impressed with mine. I was encouraged by his compliments and his assessment of our situation. I had just been taking one day at a time with God's help and doing whatever I could to get the three of us through the situation. However it was always encouraging to hear that people saw us as inspirational in the way we handle the challenges we constantly faced.

I found out in a later conversation that the night we were called over to Newcastle the team had considered carefully about operating on Emma. Apparently there were only two places who would have operated on her, one was Newcastle and the other was Canada. Obviously she wasn't well enough to fly to Canada, so Newcastle was her only hope. I believe that God was in the room when the doctors were discussing her health that night.

It seemed the whole day we were covered by the faithful prayers of friends and everything settled into place. It was a traumatic time but, compared to what we had been through, I believed things could only get better now. Shortly after breakfast I waited in a room near Ward 26 and the surgeon, Chris, who had operated on Emma came to talk to me. He explained that things had gone well and Emma would be in ITU soon. I could see her then. Shortly after he left the room, Lynne came to see me. She was the transplant co-ordinator we met when we came to Newcastle for the first assessment. We discussed the transplant, Luke's arrangements while Emma and I were away and then we went to the transplant co-ordinators office. Lynne very kindly allowed me to make a phone call so I phoned Karin, the manager of the shop where I worked back in Dublin.

We had never discussed what would happen with my job if Emma was called for transplant. It was great to hear the familiar voices from back home as I talked with Karin and Margot.

I had texted them the previous evening to tell them Emma had been called to Newcastle, they could not settle to work until they heard that she was through the operation. Everyone who came into the shop was asked to say a prayer for Emma's recovery. Karin said not to worry about time off. I had some holidays due to me and she would also talk to the area manager.

Lynne asked me if I had passports for Emma and I with me as we would be going home on a regular flight. For the past few years Emma had not been well enough to fly at the higher altitudes and any time we were called to Newcastle it was on a chartered flight.

Now with the new lungs she would be well enough to go on a short flight at the higher altitude. I would have to ask Luke to check our passports and see if they were in date. It turned out that Emma's passport was not in date. This caused endless problems. In the end I was grateful to have the help of a Sergeant who knows our family circumstances and thankfully he helped sort out Emma's new passport being issued.

The co-ordinators office was like a haven of safety. If I had any questions or just wanted someone to talk to there would always be someone in their office. Lynne arranged for me to use their mobile charger as I had forgotten mine in Thursday's drama. She also arranged for the porters to help bring my bags to the flat accommodation. She gave me directions for the conservatory if I needed somewhere peaceful to sit. This turned out to be one of my favourite places as it was a restful place and warm (which suited me perfectly as I always feel the cold). When I went back to Ward 27, two porters with good senses of humour arrived to help bring my luggage to the flats. We seemed to go through endless doors, down stairs, around corridors and at some point I thought I would never find my way back to Emma's ward. I later found my way back by following the outside wall of the hospital right the way round to the front door.

When I first saw Emma in the ITU she was lying in the bed with a sheet over her, she just looked like she was sleeping peacefully. I couldn't see tubes, lines or anything going into her. They had the room well laid out in the sense that when I walked into the room there was a window opposite. This meant that all the machines she was linked up to were not the first things I saw. Becky was the nurse looking after Emma on the first shift. She went the extra mile when nursing Emma over the next couple of days. She even washed and dried Emma's hair which is not an easy thing to do when the patient is sedated. In ITU it's 24 hour round the clock care so over the next while there would be different nurses looking after Emma as they changed their shift regularly. They do 12 hour shifts and if the patient is sedated it can be lonely for them in the ITU so they are glad when there is a relative they can talk too. I was glad of their company too. There were lots of machines monitoring different things like blood pressure, oxygen saturation and heart rate. Emma was lying there so still and I wondered if she was aware of anything or if she could hear me when I spoke to her. She looked so small on the ITU bed.

I asked if I could see what she looked like now that she had had the operation. So Becky gently pulled back the bed sheet and showed me the wound on Emma's chest where they would have opened her to take out the old lungs and put in the new ones. She showed me the tubes that were coming out of Emma's chest and talked about how these would gradually be removed as Emma recovered. Maybe it was just exhaustion but when Becky talked through these things with me, it did not seem as scary as I had imagined it would be. It was stressful that we were going through such a tough time but two things I remember from our time in Newcastle is being flooded with a huge sense of relief that the lungs had arrived in time and that every day was one step further on the road to recovery. I sat at Emma's bedside for hours watching her, listening to the sounds of the machines that were monitoring her vital signs, talking to the nurses and doctors, reading a book to pass the time and praying for her recovery.

Another thing I remember about those days was the silence. I ate my meals alone and when I took a short break from the ITU routine I had no-one to talk to. Text messages were a lifeline for me. Whenever I was out of the hospital building I would switch my mobile on and for the next minute or so lots of text messages would come through.

I got to talk to Luke later on that day. It was good to hear his voice and to hear his routine was going well. There were a few household things that I asked him to do and also to bring Emma's birthday cake to Fern and Bruce's house as we would not be back in time to eat it. I had a chat with Fern too. She said that whenever Luke wanted to talk to me he could phone from their house. She felt it was important for him to be able to contact me whenever he needed to. I later texted some friends and family and finally went to bed at 11pm. I didn't set my alarm clock as I reckoned that I would wake when I needed to. Sure enough the next morning I woke at 8am. It was a luxury to get 8 or 9 hours sleep a night after the trauma of the previous years. Often I had only been getting six hours of broken sleep a night and now I was thankful that my body was being given the chance to begin recovering.

After Emma's operation she spent the next 18 days in ITU and she was sedated for about half of that time. One of Emma's pre-transplant worries had been about the ventilation tube in her mouth. She thought it would be uncomfortable and she would feel like she was choking. After the operation it turned out that this did bother her a lot. Anytime she started coming round from the sedation she would try to move her weak arms and hands to get the tube out of her mouth. If this didn't work, she would try to use her shoulders to dislodge the tube. Sometimes she would gag quietly on the tube or cough silently. With this distressing her, it took longer for her vital signs to be stabilized and so they had to keep her sedated for longer. Although her PEG feeds did not always agree with her, they had to start these again as she was not awake to eat. One thing that impressed me was the way the doctors listened to what I said or any worries I had and they answered my questions with honesty. We had had this type of relationship with our team in Dublin and I was glad that it was the same here in Newcastle.

There was a regular stream of doctors in and out of her ITU cubicle who kept me up-to-date on her condition and reassured me that she was doing ok. Nothing seemed to take them by surprise. They always had a plan of action and followed through on it. In the early days post op, it was difficult to know how long it would be before Emma would wake up. Some people are in ITU for a few days after their transplant but Emma had been critically ill so naturally she was not expected to bounce back quickly. In the early days her progress was very slow. There seemed to be a very long road ahead in her recovery.

The daily routine quickly fell into a familiar pattern. When I woke in the mornings I would phone from my direct line in the flats to Emma's cubicle to ask the nurse how Emma had been through the night. Then I would walk from the flats to the main hospital building where the Chattery restaurant was located so I could start the day with a light breakfast. Though I was only eating because I had to. I had no interest in food, it was like cardboard in my mouth. After breakfast I would walk from the main hospital entrance over to the unit where Emma was.

When I arrived at the ITU the procedure there was to put on a plastic apron, wash my hands with water or use the hand gel, press the buzzer on the wall and wait for someone to open the door. They would phone Emma's cubicle to ask the nurse on duty if it was ok for me to go through. I spent endless hours by her bedside talking to the nurses, praying, reading books (actually got to read a book from cover to cover for the first time in years), and doing puzzle books. I would also regularly check the monitors to see how Emma was doing. We were used to watching monitors as a hospital environment had been part of our lives for so long. I knew what some of the readings were and out of curiosity I asked what the others were. Even though Emma was sedated she would still be able to hear my voice. So I would tell her things that were happening with our lives back home and who was asking for her.

As the days passed, sometimes I would sit by her bedside and wonder what it was like for her. When she is sedated does it feel like everything is happening in slow motion? Do things sound to her like they are fuzzy and far away? Is she frightened or just resting?

Sometimes I wondered if she was still with us or were the machines just keeping her body alive. At other times I would sit by her bedside willing her to wake up because I knew she would make a huge effort to recover and we could go home again. There were times when I felt very emotional thinking of all that was ahead of us in her recovery.

Dr Gerry, who was always very encouraging, said that while Emma was sedated this was my chance to have some 'me' time. When Emma woke she would need my support through her recovery. There were a few places I could go for some space and I usually took some time out when it was patients rest time in ITU between 2pm and 4pm daily.

One place I regularly went to was the conservatory located within the hospital. It was quiet and warm there and so was the perfect place to sit and read a magazine. If I wanted fresh air, I could sit outside in the September sunshine on one of the benches in the hospital grounds. These were dedicated to the memory of people who had died. On the days when I felt a bit more adventurous I would get the number 38 bus from outside the hospital to John Dobson Street in the town. Then I would spend some time browsing around the shops. I don't see myself as being a very adventurous person so I surprised myself by my efforts to explore the area we were staying in. There were beautiful walks nearby and a park across the road. On one of my trips out of the hospital I discovered a church that was only ten minutes walk from the hospital. I decided I would go there on the first Sunday morning.

When I arrived they were having their prayer meeting just inside the door of the Church. I later discovered in conversation that the minister and his wife had a relative who had had a double lung transplant. This person was seven years post transplant was now married and had a successful career. It was an encouraging story to hear particularly when Emma was still sedated in ITU. I believed this encouragement and the friendly, welcoming Church were more of God's provisions for me.

After the patients rest time each day I would go back to the ITU and stay with Emma until late at night. Then I would do the short ten minute walk to the flats at the back of the hospital. It was a quiet walk but the pathway was well lit and the area was quite open with a housing estate next to it. There was always the option of security escorting me to the flats safely if I was afraid of doing that walk late at night.

Friends and family would phone me in the flat at night time. It was so reassuring to hear their voices and to catch up on all that was happening back home. Every night Luke would phone and it was good to hear that he was doing well and being so well cared for. He would chat about school and his activities. If he knew during the day that Emma was having a test he would always text around that time to ask how it went. He was so mature about the whole experience. It was encouraging to receive texts from people to say they had seen him and he was looking well. It was great that every day he was able to go to our house to help out with checking the post for me just in case there was anything I needed to reply to. Whenever I sent Luke a text message about Emma's progress he would forward it to a circle of friends to keep them updated. The same happened when I sent a message to update friends, they would forward it to others and so we were blessed that there were lots of people everywhere praying for us.

Fern said they were happy to have Luke stay with them as long as we needed him to be there. That was so helpful because I knew he was settled within their family unit. Their house was near ours so sometimes he would go home for a while after school. He could do some of his nebulisers and then later go to Bruce and Fern's. I was very proud of him the way he was handling the whole situation with a positive attitude.

At night time I would write a short diary of what had happened that day with Emma's recovery. It's a good reminder of her daily recovery and the encouragement we got from everyone at the time. When I look back now at that diary I'm amazed that some of the major things that stand out in my mind about our experiences with Emma's transplant were not even written into the diary. I suppose that's because of the stress I was under at the time and the fact that I was recovering from all we had been through in the pre transplant days.

There always seemed to be something happening with Emma's care like the sedation being increased to help her rest more or her having a plastic radiator type blanket to keep her warm if her temperature dropped. If her white cell count went up they would do exhaustive tests to find out where the source of infection was so that it could be treated.

The longer she lay there the more her legs and stomach became swollen so the physiotherapists did regular physio sessions to move her arms and legs. Four days post transplant they decided to do a bronchoscopy. I remembered when she was younger and had a bronchoscopy. It seemed like such a big deal then because it was all new to us. Now after all we had been through it seemed like routine. So when the doctor, Tanveer, asked me if I would like to stay in the ITU cubicle while he did the bronchoscopy, I said I would like that. One thing I learned over the years of nursing Emma and Luke was that I found the world of medicine and science very interesting. My one regret to this day is that I didn't ask Tanveer if I could look down the tube to see what he could see on Emma's lungs. Tanveer said that Emma and I have been very brave to get this far, not just with the transplant but before that too.

Her ventilation was gradually changed from Bipap to Cpap with the plan being that eventually she would be progressed to bellows and then to an oxygen mask. The Bipap sends out regular breaths regardless of how the person is breathing. Cpap is set for a certain number of breaths per minute. If you do that number of breaths the machine does not need to assist your breathing. If you don't do this amount of breaths the machine will do it for you.

We had built up a good rapport with the team from the oxygen company back in Dublin. I knew they would want to know how Emma's recovery was going. I texted Keith with the settings on Emma's machines. His replies eased my worries because I knew he knew what those settings meant. He would text back encouraging messages that would say things like, if she is on those settings she is doing well. Months later, he admitted that if I had texted settings that were not good he was not sure how, or if, he would have replied.

When Emma's vital signs were more stable they were going to put a tracheotomy tube in rather than the ventilation tube. This would be less distressing for her. On this same day, although Emma couldn't open her eyes as she was so heavily sedated, she was able to squeeze my hand in answer to my questions and it was encouraging to know that she could hear me and respond.

Mostly, the days were lonely. I found it hard to be interested in food. I needed company more. I missed my friends and my life back home. I didn't know when I would see them again. My parents, sister and brothers kept in touch by phone and text. My brother, Alan, had offered to come over to Newcastle so I would not be facing all of this alone. I valued his offer but asked instead if he would bring Luke over some weekend soon. The rest of the family also planned to bring Luke over on separate weekends so I was looking forward to all of those trips.

Our minister and friend, Alan, kept in regular contact and relayed news of Emma's progress back to our Church family. It meant so much to have their support and care for us during this traumatic time.

Emma's school have always been very supportive of us through Emma's health issues and often went the extra mile. While we were in Newcastle, Emma's year leader gave Luke lifts to school. The morning after we were called for Emma's transplant I was so touched by his thoughtfulness. I heard, that he gave Luke a note to bring to all his classes to let the teachers know that he was allowed to keep his mobile phone on in class just in case I needed to get in touch with him. It was comforting to know that at this time when I couldn't be at home with Luke, friends were looking out for him.

One of Emma's teachers, Heather, gave me the number of her sister who lived near Newcastle. Her sister, Thelma, kindly gave up some of her time to come to the hospital. We would drive somewhere nearby for coffee and a chat. I really appreciated those times. It was much later she told me that the first time she saw Emma she, as a trained nurse, was shocked at how unwell Emma looked. I know I was looking at things from a different perspective. I had nursed Emma for the whole year before this. No matter how bad things looked post transplant, they were so much better than what we had been through. I felt that every day since the transplant, things could only improve, she was on the road to recovery now.

There was a great buzz at the hospital Emma had been attending in Dublin. Ger, our Nurse Specialist, was in contact by text and phoned every few days to see how Emma was recovering. Many of the nurses on Oak Ward had become special to us in the year before Emma's transplant. One of them was Ger C and we kept in touch while Emma and I were in Newcastle. Any time she went onto the ward where the nurses, kitchen staff, playroom people, playroom visitors, assistant matron and the art teacher all knew Emma so well, they were eager to hear about Emma's recovery. Karin and Margot, from my workplace, were asking how things were. Customers and staff from the nearby shops used to call in for updates on how Emma was progressing.

I kept in touch with Suzanne from the CF Research Trust. I knew she would want to know how Emma was doing in her recovery. Emma had done a lot of fundraising for CFRT while she was in hospital. The night she was going in for the transplant Emma was disappointed that by the time she got back to Dublin it might be too late to sell the calendar that had been printed up to raise funds for CFRT. However, while she was still sedated in ITU, Luke and some friends back home were selling the calendar and with the support of everyone this calendar helped to raise thousands for CFRT.

I also had a phone call from the Cystic Fibrosis Association. They had heard about Emma's call for transplant and were enquiring about her recovery.

James, a friend of ours, also texted to find out how Emma was doing. He had been so helpful to Emma in her pre transplant days when she had questions and worries about a transplant. As he had been through the experience many years previously he was able to reassure her with answers to her questions.

We heard that the neighbourhood was buzzing with the excitement of hearing that Emma got her transplant in time. My friends from our neighbourhood would phone regularly to see how things were going with Emma's progress and they also helped out with lifts for Luke.

This is what Luke remembers about us being in Newcastle:

When the transplant call came for Emma it was a big shock. I never thought the call was going to come but when it did all these questions just went though my mind such as: What's going to happen to me now that they have to go? Will Emma make it? Will the lungs be compatible?

I also was very happy that this could be a new life for all of us. After the call everything just happened in fast motion. Mum was in the middle of cooking our dinner so I was told to eat my dinner and that Fern would collect me soon to bring me to their house to look after me. The ambulance came within a few minutes to bring them to England which attracted a crowd of our neighbours.

When Mum and Emma left in the ambulance, a few of the lads from the road came in and kept me company for a while and just made sure that I was ok. That was great as it took my mind off what was happening which I needed. I then went to the house that I was going to stay in till Emma and Mum came home. It was going to be weird without Mum and Emma around but it was grand cause I was amongst friends.

15

Recovery Time

At the beginning of the second week Emma was still sedated. One of the Consultants came to see how Emma was doing but also to talk to me. He said that Emma was better than she had been but there was still a long road ahead. Some people wake faster than others after the operation. The doctors were keeping a close eye on her. At this point the trachea tube was in place. She was on minimal ventilation so the plan would be to move her onto bellows and then an oxygen mask over the tracheotomy tube. Then, in time, she would be transferred to the ward. She had some movement but was not responding to commands.

Sometimes I would find it hard to get motivated in the mornings. I couldn't always face breakfast in the hospital restaurant so I would snack on a piece of fruit or cereal bar in my room at the flats. It was very lonely so the text messages from home continued to be a source of encouragement to me. A text can mean so much at times like that.

A friend would say that he felt strongly in his spirit and soul that Emma is going to make it.

Another friend would say they hoped it wouldn't be too long before she comes round and then I would be able to speak to her. He knew that is what I missed and encouraged me to keep my head up. Someone else would text to say the grapevine of love, concern and prayer is working well. Another friend would say they couldn't even start to imagine what we are going through. They were thinking of us and so were their friends and family. We had regular contact with our CF team back in Dublin.

We had encouraging messages from the nurses on Oak Ward who had nursed Emma. The team at the oxygen company also kept in regular contact. Every day I would send an updated text message of Emma's progress that day and this text was forwarded to many concerned friends. I felt we were being carried by the prayers of the army of people who were praying for us.

By now friends had the address of the hospital and it was lovely to receive cards and letters of support and encouragement.

My brother, Alan, brought Luke over to Newcastle eight days after Emma had her transplant. Luke was a bit concerned about how Emma would look when he saw her. He had a long conversation with the school nurse the day before he came to Newcastle about the plans for his trip and what he imagined Emma would be like. I reassured him too that Emma just looked like she was asleep. I explained the wires and tubes coming out of her were just like other times he would have seen her at the hospital except this time there were more than usual. There were some spare rooms available at the flat accommodation at the back of the hospital and the transplant co-ordinators very kindly gave us the keys for one of the rooms that Luke and Alan could stay in. I had told Luke that I hoped I didn't get all emotional when I saw him and cry on his shoulder. So when they arrived the next morning, he called from a distance "Now don't get all emotional". He is such a tonic or humour and positivity.

Unfortunately Luke had a cold and so he could not be allowed near Emma in case he gave her an infection. This meant Luke had to stay in the airlock between the ward and Emma's room which was a bit boring for him. Emma responded to Alan's voice and for the hour or so that he was there she had plenty of movement in her arms and legs. Her eyes were slightly open and she tried to open them further. She lifted her arms once and even managed a silent yawn.

It wasn't fair to make Luke wait in the airlock for too long and the car magazine I bought for him only kept him entertained for a short while. So after a while we headed into the city on the bus. While we were there I bought him a present to congratulate him on his Junior Cert exam results he had just received.

When we got back to the unit later on, Emma was doing very well with her movements. One of the nurses, Katie, spent time talking to Luke and explaining things about Emma's condition. It was great to have Alan and Luke there for the day and I especially enjoyed their company for meals and talking.

Before I went back to the flats I explained to Emma that Alan and Luke would come and say goodbye in the morning before they left for their early morning flight. It was strange that night in my flat knowing they were in the flat below mine but when I woke they would be gone back to Dublin. I wanted to freeze those moments in time so they would be there when I woke up. Or if I couldn't do that then I wished Emma and I could go home with them, back to our lives, back to everything familiar. Instead I had to be brave and stay longer in Newcastle. I did not want to go back to the loneliness of the routine that had become normality in the previous week. I wanted to be at home with my friends, my family, my Church, my job, my life.

The next day Emma seemed to have more movement. She was responding more to sounds and voices. Her blood pressure increased when I walked into the room. The nurse said this was because Emma recognized my voice. Emma had more control over her movements and her eyes were open a little more. Tanveer showed me some exercises I could do to help relieve the fluid which had built up under her eyelids and this in turn would make it easier for Emma to open her eyes. If I asked Emma a question she would squeeze my hand to let me know the answer. They were still trying to find the cause of her temperature but nothing conclusive had come back from microbiology yet. Otherwise than that her signs are stable.

Although Emma had seemed to take a step forward with movement in her arms, legs and eyes, later in the day she had an episode that set her back. The doctor on duty, took the time to explain why that might have happened and he reassured me that she would be ok.

They gave her a longer acting sedative so she would sleep for a few hours. I was worn out by the multitude of emotions that I faced that afternoon so as she was going to be sedated for a while I decided I would go out and get some much needed fresh air.

The next day Emma was much improved. She was propped up in bed with her eyes half open. She was able to respond to commands and did her best to communicate. Unfortunately with the trachea tube in place, there was no sound to her voice. We had to resort to yes/no questions. At one point after going through an exhaustive list of questions it turned out she wanted me to hug her. I did my best to hug her allowing for all the tubes that were connected to her. Before her transplant when she was critically ill, at times she had not been able for hugs because her lungs were too sore. Or even just touching her back or rubbing her back would make her cough up mucus. It was a positive sign that she was able for hugs again.

As the week progressed Emma was able to be changed from the Cpap to the bellows. This was progress. The thought struck me that that the doctors, Tanveer, Jagan, Jim and the rest of the team, who had been so supportive to me over the past week or so are strangers to her as she was only getting to meet them now. Chris the surgeon who had done the transplant visited Emma. He told me there is a long road ahead in her recovery.

As I mentioned earlier in the book, Emma never liked physiotherapy. Early in this week the physiotherapists did some leg exercises with Emma and when they said they would return later that day for some more, Emma threw her eyes up to Heaven. I smiled as I thought…our Emma is back. Her character was starting to shine through again.

Later on in the week they were able to hoist her out of the bed into a chair beside the bed. She seemed to like sitting in the chair. As she was small for her age she kept sliding down the bed because of the angle it was at and also it was an adult size bed. By the end of the week they had her standing with the help of a zimmer frame. They were trying to get her to do some marching on the spot to bring down the swelling in her legs and help to get her active again. She was asked to do ten steps but she was determined to do more. Her feet were swollen and sore but she managed to do thirty steps.

We were now going into our second week in Newcastle and the realities of day to day living were beginning to kick in. I needed to do some laundry but the launderette at the flats was closed for repairs. I found out some information about local launderettes and set off on my journey. Between walking, arriving at the launderette that was no longer open, stopping for lunch, finding a launderette that was open, doing the laundry, more walking and then getting the bus back to the hospital, it all took about five hours. My brother, Alan, said there is no need to go to the gym over there, just do the laundry every day and that would keep me fit. Thankfully the launderette by the flats was reopened within the next week.

When I got back to the hospital later I was met with the news that they were giving me a flat mate. Although I was initially not looking forward to this, it turned out that my flat mate and I got on very well. We had similar routines and times for going to and from the hospital. Her husband had been in for heart surgery so she would only be in the accommodation for a few days.

As we headed into Emma's third week of recovery there were times when progress seemed slow with one or two setbacks. There were also other times when she came on in leaps and bounds. At times she was tired, pale and found it too uncomfortable to sit on the chair at the side of the bed, so she would ask to stay in bed. Or if she did sit out in the chair she needed a heat pack to help with the pain in her back. It was heartbreaking to watch. She had been through so much already and I wished a speedier recovery for her. She wanted me to be with her as much as possible.

When it came to the ITU rest time for the patients in the afternoon, she reluctantly let me go. If I was late back she would tap her watch as if to ask where had I been. She had steps of progress with the ventilation and did very well with her breathing.

We were still trying to communicate by us asking yes and no questions. She tried writing what she wanted to say on a page but her hands were still very weak which made holding the pen difficult. As she became stronger and started to write things, it became easier to communicate but sometimes what she wrote didn't make sense to us. It was about hallucinations she had had or about the dream she had the night of the transplant, so it only made sense to her. Once or twice she would make strange faces and motion towards the corner of the ITU cubicle as if she saw something horrible there.

Later we discovered that part of her hallucinations was seeing spiders on the ceiling. It was a confusing time for Emma. She had been sedated for eight days and now that she was coming round she had to deal with so much change. When she saw the nurses preparing her medicine, she would want me to tell them what medication she was on but,of course, it had all changed now. In time we would have to learn the new medication regime.

One time she communicated to me that the next time Luke was coming to visit her in the hospital, she would like him to bring a particular thing from her room. I realized then that she thought she was still in Dublin. I gently explained to her that we were in the hospital in Newcastle. I knew by her reaction that she was not happy to be away from home. I think this feeling of wanting to be back where everything was familiar added to her determination to have as quick a recovery as possible. This was evident in the effort she put into her progress over the next while.

When the physiotherapists came to do the daily exercises, Emma would push herself to do more than they asked. They had a zimmer frame to help her stand. Her ankles looked like they would burst with all the fluid that had built up because of inactivity while she was sedated. When they first tried to help her up to a standing position with the zimmer frame, she pulled herself up into a standing position. She continued to do more steps than they asked. She was also still being hoisted out of bed in the morning to sit on the bedside chair. Part way through the week she stood with help, turned around and sat on the bed. Another step forward.

They did a swallow test to see if any of the liquid was going onto her lungs. She was then allowed some orange juice. When that was successful she progressed to ice cream.

Earlier in the week, Emma had communicated about going home.She was anxious about the flight being at the higher altitude than she had been used to in the past couple of years.

She was afraid that her lungs would collapse. I reassured her that they would not send her on the flight if they thought this was going to happen. They had put a lot of effort and time into her operation and recovery and would not doing anything to put her at risk. She started to ask questions about whose lungs she had been given. So we agreed to ask the transplant co-ordinator they next time we saw her.

Mid week there was some talk of Emma going to ward 27a which would be the next step forward in her recovery. When it did not happen on the day they had mentioned, Emma was very disappointed. So Jagan, who was on duty that day, compromised by telling Emma she could go to the hospital shop to have a change of scene from the ITU. She was put into a wheelchair, linked up to the oxygen and her entourage of me and two nurses (one with an emergency tracea kit) escorted her along the hospital corridors to the shop. She was delighted for this short glimpse of normality. A female customer in the shop was sad to see the state of Emma's small frame, wheelchair bound and on oxygen and I didn't have the energy to tell her that this was Emma in recovery.

The following day Emma was moved to the ward. I had heard from the ITU nurses that when someone is moving from ITU to the ward all the nurses and doctors line up to say goodbye to them as they are wheeled out of ITU. I hoped they would give me some notice of when this was happening because it would be a very emotional moment leaving the care of ITU and going to the ward. They had all been so fantastic I didn't want to think of saying goodbye to them even though it was good to move on to the next stage of Emma's recovery.

This is what Luke remembers about the time when Emma and I were in Newcastle.

Everything was organized. I would get a lift into school with Andrew, then later I would be collected by a neighbour and brought home where I would do homework and other things around the house. Later Fern would collect me and bring me back to their house. It was very different to my usual routine but I got used to it.

The night that Mum and Emma went to Newcastle I stayed up till I heard if Emma was going to get the lungs or not. One of the daughters of the family that I was staying with waited up as well and just before I was going to go to bed I heard that Emma got the lungs.

It was weird at first not having Emma and Mum not around but I got used to it and I was talking to Mum most nights on the phone so that made it better. Everyone was so supportive and offered to help me whenever I needed it. That made this time while Emma and Mum were in Newcastle a lot easier.

16

Leaps and Bounds

With Emma on the ward it seemed like her progress sped up. Jagan and another doctor changed her trachea tube for a thinner one. She now had a speaking valve so we could hear her speak. Her first word was 'Hello'. I had thought she was going to ask for her favourite food as she had been asking about it last week.

On her first night in the ward Emma asked if she could stay on the trachea mask and not have the bellows unless it was absolutely necessary. The nurse agreed. Emma continued to make lots of effort as she was so determined to recover and get home.

I had texted Luke with the direct line telephone number for the cubicle Emma was staying in on the ward. His routine now seemed to be that a friend of ours would collect Luke from school as she worked nearby. She would bring him home to our house and he would spend some time at our house checking the post and making himself some snacks to eat. He would phone me from either our home or from Fern's every day. It was easier now that we had a direct line into Emma's room as before this I would have to agree a time with him and then come out of the hospital building to switch on my mobile so I could take his calls. Or if we missed out on that mobile call, we would have to wait until the evening before we could talk with each other. Later in the afternoon Fern or a friend would bring Luke to Fern and Bruce's house.

The day after Emma moved to the ward the trachea tube was taken out. A dressing was put over the wound and it should start to knit over the next few days. Tanveer took the time to talk through any worries she had It seemed like her progress was coming in leaps and bounds as she was taken off different equipment she had been linked up to.

She could now walk from her bed to the ensuite bathroom but sometimes when walking she needed my help as her legs would go weak. She was expected to take her meds orally now and in time would be taught all about her new medicines. She was also able to feed herself again. It was amazing to see her doing simple things that she was not able to do for so long like laughing without choking on her mucus.

One of the transplant co-ordinators called to see us and told us about the donor. She told us that the donor's family would have known that a young girl from Ireland got their child's lungs. It was sad to imagine what they were going through and I was aware for each week of Emma's recovery, they were a week further into grieving for their child who had died. We were told we could write a letter to the donor's family at any time and the co-ordinator would pass it on to them. So I decided I would do this before we went home to Dublin. If Emma had not been called for the transplant she would, at this stage, possibly be dying with only days left to go.

One night I was standing at the doors of the hospital in Newcastle waiting for our Chinese take away to arrive. In the time that I was standing there waiting, I saw some of the transplant team loading up a van with equipment they needed. They must have got a call to say there were organs available and they had to go and check them out. I was standing there thinking, with great admiration, of all the behind the scenes work they have to do to match up the organs with a suitable recipient and organise the patients transport to the hospital.

It was difficult being away from home particularly on days when Luke was not feeling well. The second day after Emma had been transferred to the ward, Luke phoned and was feeling a bit miserable with a head cold. I was trying to talk to him about getting to bed on time particularly on school nights but I wasn't getting too far with that advice.

One of the doctors in the room at the time was good humoured. So I handed the phone to him and he told Luke to go to bed on time and take paracetamol regularly.

I was touched by the kindness of people who sent cards, supported and encouraged us and who took the time to come over to see us. One of the first people to visit was my friend, Marg, who came over for a day when Emma was in ITU. I appreciated her company for the day.

When people sent a text message I imagined them in the setting I knew them from and it helped to have a picture in my mind of home. One of these text messages was from Valerie. She was part of the team of play therapists at the hospital. She texted to say, 'I know Emma is strong because she has lots of love and support from you and visa versa…take care x x'

I would remember the times in the past when the team of play therapists would regularly visit Emma in her hospital room. They would spend time talking with her and catching up on her news.

I would imagine Karin and Margot in the card shop we worked in. They had told me that regular customers were asking how Emma was doing. Staff from the surrounding shops in the centre wanted to be kept up to date on Emma's progress and I realized that our shopping centre was not just a place of work. It was community who cared about each other.

It meant so much that the text messages were still coming regularly from family and friends at home, from Alan and our friends in Church, from our hospital family and also to have friends and family helping out with Luke. The phone calls continued coming to the flat at night time when I had returned there after a day at the hospital with Emma. It was always great to hear news from home.

During the week there were times when Emma had to have tests as part of the recovery process. One day she had been booked in for a CT scan. She had to drink lots of a horrible tasting liquid and all this fluid going into her caused her discomfort on her lungs.

After the scan, Emma was crying and asking me why she still can not breathe as well as she thought she would be able to. I didn't have an answer as this was all new territory to me as well. We just had to be patient in this time of recovery and be thankful for every step towards her new quality of life. She told me she was glad she got the transplant even though her recovery was slower than she had imagined it would be.

Nearer the end of the week Emma had extensive tests to find out the cause of her temperature. The result showed an infection in her system so this was immediately treated with antibiotics. It was quite a stressful week with all these tests being performed. This was also the week I was trying to sort out an up to date passport for Emma.

We had been looking forward to the weekend of Emma's third week over there as my brother, Philip, was bringing Luke over to see us. They had had a very early start to get to Dublin Airport for their flight so the first thing we did when they arrived was have breakfast at the hospital restaurant. When we went to spend some time with Emma she was not in good form. Unfortunately for Luke, he was not allowed into her cubicle again as he still had an infection and was on oral antibiotics. There was a parent's room that Luke could sit in and I divided my time between being there with him and spending time in Emma's room. It was not really fair to Luke to have to spend endless hours in the parents room so after a while Luke, Philip and I went to town for something to eat.

When we arrived back at the hospital later, Luke gave me his laptop to give to Emma. He had made a short recording of get well wishes from friend's back home for Emma. When we went back to the flats later I had that same sinking feeling that tomorrow Luke and Philip would be going back home.

The next morning I got up early to say goodbye to them and to get their flat keys to give back to the co-ordinator later in the day. After I said goodbye to them I stood in the quietness and darkness of the early morning watching until the taxi lights were out of sight. I wondered how long it would be before Emma and I would be in a taxi heading towards the airport to go home.

The next day Emma was in better form. When she had been unwell before her transplant, there were no expectations on her to participate in everyday life as her main task everyday was breathing. I noticed that now in her recovery time she tended to put things on the long finger. She bargained with everyday tasks. She would agree to do something partly but not completely. I had a chat with her and explained how she needed to co-operate so she could get the best out of her recovery.

After our talk I washed her hair while she sat in the shower. She felt much better afterwards and decided she would try walking along the corridor. One of the nurses followed us with a wheelchair in case Emma needed it. I carried the small oxygen tank and Emma linked my arm as we walked along the corridor.

She surprised us all by walking three times farther than we thought she would. She was so brave. Her ankles were still swollen and sore. Her goal seemed to be to get to the lifts and when we reached there she asked the nurse if we could go to the hospital shop. The nurse agreed, so Emma and I headed off to the shop with Emma in the wheelchair as it was too far to walk.

Later when we got back to the ward Emma walked slowly from the entrance of the ward to her cubicle. The nurses were very impressed with her. She went for another walk later that night. She said her lungs were fine, it's just her feet and stomach that are still painful because they are swollen. I bought some foot soak in a chemist earlier in the week. It helps Emma to soak her feet in a basin of water for a while and then I massage some cream into her feet. I also bought her a pair of soft slippers but her feet were too swollen to fit into them and they kept falling off. We tried out different slippers and footwear but nothing was successful until the swelling went down.

She made another step forward as her oxygen level was reduced further. Although it sounds like an easy step forward it was more difficult than it sounds. Before the operation, Emma had become used to knowing that she had the oxygen to help her breathe. It was a huge psychological step to allow the oxygen level to be reduced. The nurses had told me that the doctors had said it was ok for Emma's oxygen to be reduced but that every time they mentioned it to Emma she got upset. I knew the only way to get past this point was to reduce the oxygen level without Emma seeing it being reduced.

She would get used to breathing with the lower level of oxygen and then I would later be able to tell her she had been on that for a while. She would know then that it was safe for the level to be reduced. So that's what I did. Hours later when she had had no problems with the new level, I told Emma about the progress she had made. She said nothing for a moment but then realized that she was ok on the new level of oxygen. More steps forward.

In week four we had a similar situation to face in her recovery when the doctors told her that shortly she would not need the oxygen at all. She burst out crying. I found over the next while that the psychological readjustment after transplant was one of the most challenging parts of her recovery. She had become used to having the oxygen to help her breathe and the initial suggestion of being without it was a scary thought. She made a giant step forward in her recovery at the beginning of this week. She wanted to go for another walk along the corridor. The more exercise she did, the quicker the swelling would go down on ankles and stomach. I encouraged her to try walking without the oxygen and wheelchair. Although she was reluctant to do this at first, she agreed to it and did brilliantly.

The physiotherapists would daily go through exercises with Emma either on the ward or in the hospital gym. In the gym she could do steps, the bicycle, and sit/stand-ups.

During this fourth week, Emma was introduced to the names and daily doses of her new medicines. She would have to take anti-rejection drugs for the rest of her life. Initially she would be on 15 different medications taken at different intervals during the day which amounted to 32 doses of medicine daily. Over time and on the advice of her doctor, she would discontinue some and others would be added or changed.

Midweek we had a visit from some friends from Dublin. Alan, our minister and friend who had been in touch every day since we had come over to Newcastle for Emma's transplant. Also two friends, Diane and Hilary. I appreciated the time they all took out of their busy schedules to come over to see us.

The day before they came had been stressful so it was great to spend time relaxing with them and enjoying their company.

The day blended together so well. We spent time talking about news from home as we sat in the room with Emma. We shared meals together and went into town for a while.

Later I got to introduce them to Dr. Gerry, who had been so encouraging and positive in his conversations with us.

Emma had to have a new treatment that day. Back home my Mother accompanied Luke to hospital as he had some tests and a check up. I found it difficult being away from home because I wanted to be there for him too.

Before our friends went back to Dublin, Alan, our minister, did a lovely communion service in Emma's cubicle. It was very special. Diane made a short video of Emma and I sending greetings to our friends in our Church back home. They would play this on the overhead after the Sunday service.

As I was talking and Diane was recording, I imagined our friends listening to and looking at this short video and I felt very choked up with a lump in my throat and tears in my eyes. I wanted to be there with them, I missed them all.

Later when Alan, Diane and Hilary were going home, I walked over to the taxi with them. I was sad to see them go. Although I had kept a type of journal of Emma's progress and encouraging messages since we arrived in Newcastle, I didn't write in it for the three days after they left because I was homesick.

More friends visited at the weekend. Two friends came on Saturday night and stayed until Sunday morning and then two more friends came on Sunday morning for the day. I noticed that every visit was enjoyable in different ways. It was great to have the company of friends to talk with and have meals with.

At the start of the fifth week, Emma's progress continued. The physiotherapists had a goal that she had to complete before being discharged from the hospital. She had to walk up a flight of stairs. They would try this slowly by starting off with 3 steps. Emma managed this and later in the day she wanted to try the whole flight of stairs. Again she excelled by doing two flights of stairs.

In the initial stages of her recovery she was not bothered about checking her mobile messages but in this fifth week she began showing an interest in checking her messages again. I saw this as more progress.

The nurses and pharmacist did some medicine education training with us as Emma would not be discharged from the hospital until she was fully au fait with all her medicines. We were on a learning curve. Whereas I had done her medicine regime before the transplant now she was considered to be under adult care and responsible for taking her own medicine. I found this to be a huge readjustment as I had been so used to being her carer particularly since she had been 24 hour care for the past year.

Emma had an outpatients appointment at the end of the week and as they were happy with her progress, the Consultant decided to discharge her to the flats. Whereas all the accommodation they had given me was in upstairs flats, Emma and I would now be in a downstairs flat. It was a larger one and self contained. The idea of being discharged to the flats is that the patient gets to experience life outside the hospital but they still have the back up of the hospital should they need it.

My Mum, sister, niece, Luke and a friend of ours were all over that weekend. It would be Luke's 16th birthday the following week. He had been very patient over the past few years as with Emma's health had celebrated some of his birthdays by her hospital bed. We had even set off the hospital fire alarm one year with the heat of the birthday candles on his cake. Since he would be in Dublin for his birthday this year and we would be in England, I decided to take him out for a treat while he was visiting us in Newcastle. He is passionate about football so we went to St. James Park and I bought him the Newcastle jersey. We also went to the training ground for Newcastle and two of the trainers got permission to allow us to stand at the far end of the field to watch the team training. We brought back Chinese take away to Emma's cubicle.

The next day all of our group helped us to move Emma's belongings from her cubicle to the flats. The co-ordinators had given us a key for one of the upstairs flats for two of the group who were over. The local minister and his wife had very kindly agreed to put up three of our group in their house.

When Emma was being discharged from hospital, I felt there had been three very definite stages of her recovery.

The first was in ITU when she had 24 hour around the clock care.

The second stage was moving to the ward for more of her recovery and also learning to become a little more independent but with some nursing care.

The third stage was being discharged from hospital and learning to live with post transplant care. As Emma was being discharged from the hospital, I watched her chatting to the nurses.

The transplant was such a miracle. It was incredible to think that only five weeks prior to this she was critically ill, could hardly breathe and was wheelchair bound. Now she was able to walk along the ward with us smiling and talking. Her feet still hurt her when she was walking but in time this would sort itself out.

It was strange being in the flats at first. Emma was understandably anxious and kept wondering if she should phone the ward to check medication with the nurses. Everything about Emma's pre transplant care was familiar but now we had to learn about life post transplant.

I was glad we had the company of family and friends over that weekend. When they left to go home, I hoped it would not be long before we would be making our journey home.

Sometimes just to have a change from the loneliness and boredom, I would get a wheelchair and wheel Emma from the flats over to the main hospital. We would leave the wheelchair there hoping it would be there when we got back (so we could transport Emma back to the flats in it.). Then we would get the bus to either the town centre or to the shopping centre about an hour's journey away.

Emma was not able to walk much but the change of environment did us good.

17

Seventy Blessings

One night when Emma and I were in the flat, I noticed that she was walking around the flat and her breathing was so quiet compared to what it had been like before the transplant. I thought about the difference the transplant had made to her. I decided that while I was sitting there I would make a list of all the blessings we had received during our time in Newcastle. Here is the list I wrote at that time…

1. The day we were called for her operation she had not been hungry as she was so ill. So she was basically fasting for an operation before we knew the call would come.

2. We were at home by ourselves when the call came for transplant. This meant no emotional farewells which although it would have been nice to have the support, it would possibly have been too much to deal with.

3. We were at home when the call came through. If Emma had been in hospital and I had to come home, pack and get back to her at the hospital, it would have been added stress.

4. Our open house for Emma's birthday was cancelled which meant we all had a quieter afternoon in preparation of what was ahead.

5. She had rested for the afternoon before being called for transplant so she was not overtired for the operation.

6. Friends were here to say goodbye with Luke and to take his mind off Emma and I being whisked away in the ambulance.

7. There was accommodation on the hospital site for me for 5 weeks.

8. There was accommodation for family and friends when they came to visit as the flats were not too busy at those times.

9. There was a flat for Emma and me to stay in post op. These had only been re-opened in the previous few months.

10. The night of the operation, the timing was perfect in that it was 7pm and there was not much traffic on the roads. This made it easier both in Dublin and in Newcastle for the ambulance to get to the airport or hospital.

11. Weather conditions, on the night we were called for transplant, were perfect which meant a calm flight. There

was a beautiful red sky at the Airport as we waited for the plane to take us to Newcastle. During the flight, there was a beautiful full moon which shimmered across the calm sea below us.

12. The Hospital in Newcastle was the centre of excellence. There was a fantastic team of consultants, doctors and nurses.

13. In some other countries the patient or family of the patient have to fund raise. Thankfully this was not so for us as it would have added unbelievable stress to an already stressful situation.

14. The night of the transplant the doctors had carefully considered operating on Emma. Thankfully they went ahead with the operation that gave her back quality of life.

15. Nurses gave her excellent care.

16. Dr. Gerry was very positive and encouraging in all the conversations we had with him. He left the hospital to start a new job in a different hospital two weeks after we left Newcastle to come home. If we had been called any other time, he would not have been there when we were there.

17. All household bills and paperwork were up to date before we had to go to Newcastle.

18. Lungs arrived just in time, another few weeks and Emma would have been too ill for the operation.

19. Lovely hospital which has facilities like the Chattery restaurant, hairdressers, shop, library, pharmacy, conservatory, and a taxi service directly outside the hospital.

20. When Emma came through the sedation, she made steps of progress every day.

21. No rejection on her first bronchoscopy.

22. Newly transplanted patient lives 15 minutes away from us in Ireland so if Emma wanted to she could get in touch with this girl and they may be a support for each other.

23. Got to read a book from cover to cover. Cannot remember how long it is since I had the time to do that.

24. Emma's anti-rejection drugs were changed from one which caused awful side effects to one which had less side effects.

25. Emma is actively involved in her new medication regime.

26. Emma is able to walk with no oxygen or wheelchair back up.

27. Emma's appetite has returned.

28. Emma can laugh again without bringing up loads of mucus.

29. A huge sense that prayers were constantly being answered and that God was going ahead of us preparing every step.

30. Emma's dreams and hopes for the future were restored. Sitting in her cubicle one day she started talking about what career she would like to do when she leaves school.

31. As Emma's health deteriorated, our lives blended into one. Now we will all have a new quality of life.

32. I got over to the flats safely every night.

33. Emma came through the operation safely even though she had been so poorly beforehand.

34. Emma got the lungs of a person younger than her so she feels that she has been given longer time than if she got the lungs of someone her own age.

35. Emma's recovery was different than others who suffered some initial rejection of the organs they had received and needed extra treatment.

36. The team at the hospital are just a phone call away.

37. Bruce and Fern welcomed Luke into their family for the six weeks we were away.

38. People were able to help out with lifts to school for Luke every day.

39. Andrew gave Luke a note so he could keep his mobile on in class in case I needed to contact him.

40. Luke had been used to our routine with Emma in hospital so often he reverted back to that while we were in

Newcastle. It was like as if the pre transplant days had prepared him for when we were in England.

41. An army of people were praying for us in family, friends and Church.

42. Encouragement and support from home while we were in Newcastle.

43. People kind and thoughtful.

44. Cards from home to let us know people were thinking of us.

45. Visit from a friend. It was great to have her company for the day.

46. Visit from 3 friends. The day before they came had been very stressful so it was great to spend time relaxing with them.

47. Visit from two friends. Lovely to spend the day with them.

48. Visit from two more friends. Lovely to have their company for the day.

49. My brother Alan brought Luke over to Newcastle. They were our first visitors. It was great to have their company.

50. My brother Philip brought Luke over to Newcastle. Great to have them there with us.

51. My mother, sister, niece, friend and Luke all came to visit. It was great to have them over to visit. They were also there to help us move Emma from the ward to the flat.

52. Emma's calendars selling well while we were away and lots of money was raised for CF Research.

53. Phone calls from home.

54. Luke was looking after the post that was delivered to home. If anything important came in he would tell me so I could deal with it.

55. We had help in sorting out Emma's passport.

56. Beautiful bouquet of flowers sent by friends which brightened up the flat as they were not allowed in the ITU.

57. Emma and Luke's school were so supportive and caring. Also one of the teachers there put me in touch with her sister who lived about half an hour away from the hospital in Newcastle. Thelma often came to the hospital and we would have coffee and a chat. I really appreciated the time she took out of her busy schedule to drive to the hospital and spend time with me while we were going through the tough days of Emma's recovery.

58. Our inspiring story of courage is being used by God to touch people's lives.

59. Mum accompanied Luke to his hospital appointment while I as in England.

60. Daily texts that meant a lot.

61. Emma's call for transplant came at the beginning of the school year and not during exams time.

62. Call for transplant came during school term time so it meant that Luke could be kept in his routine. I believe at a time like that routine is important for keeping some kind of normality in the situation.

63. Lots of encouraging text messages from family and friends.

64. Encouraging text messages from our friends at our hospital back in Dublin and from Keith from the Oxygen company. It meant a lot knowing they had medical background and were able to give words of reassurance.

65. Text messages from lots of people who were praying for us.

66. Text messages from unexpected people and from people who took the time to text when they were on their holidays.

67. Daily strength to cope with our situation.

68. Friendly and welcoming Church nearby where the minister and his wife had an encouraging story of someone in their family who had had a successful double lung transplant seven years earlier. Minister and his wife offered overnight accommodation to Mum, my sister and Luke when they came to visit. They also offered accommodation to Emma and I when Emma would have to return for Biopsy visits at 3 months, 6 months and 12 months post transplant.

69. The hospital in Newcastle was in a nice part of the city. There was a park across the road and the hospital was within walking distance of local places. Also the hospital had a good bus service which went from outside the door to the town. The people of Newcastle were so friendly. They deserve the award they won for being the friendliest city.

70. The cost of living was cheaper over in Newcastle.

When we went to the Outpatients clinic on the Friday morning, the Consultant was so pleased with Emma's progress that he said we could go home.

If we wanted wheelchair assistance at the Airport we would have to wait for a Saturday flight as a wheelchair could not be organized for the Friday night. We were so keen to go home that we decided we would do without wheelchair assistance. So they booked our flights for the Friday.

Packing turned out to be quite a challenge as we had brought some of her medicines and her nebuliser with us. We also had a month's supply of her new medicines, 6 weeks of clothes and living items to pack into our bags.

We were delighted to be going home but we were both apprehensive in different ways.

Emma was upset as she had not traveled on a regular flight for a long time as she had been too unwell. In clinic that day the nurse kindly explained to Emma that they would not send her on a regular flight if they thought that anything would happen to her new lungs.

I was nervous at the thought of getting through Airport security with all her medicines. There were limits on liquids allowed on board at the time and we had so much medicine to bring home I wondered if we would have hassle getting it through security checks.

As it happened when we arrived at security with about four pieces of hand luggage between us, the young security man said 'Ah Flower, you have too many bags, you will have to go back to check in and put some in the hold'. I explained to him that these were important medications for Emma as she was post double lung transplant. I explained that we could not risk these getting damaged in the hold or lost as that would put her health at risk.

As with so many other situations that I had faced over many years, even though I felt afraid I had to be strong because the situation demanded that of me. All I could do was pray about it and trust God to get us through. Thankfully the information about Emma being post double lung transplant seemed to put him at a loss for words and he just put the bags on the conveyor belt and allowed us through to the next part of the security check. The security supervisor on the far side of the conveyor belt just asked us to open our bags and take out some of the liquid medicines so he could see that they had hospital labels on them. He also read the short letter from the hospital explaining the necessity of carrying these medications and then he very kindly asked how Emma was doing since the transplant. The other reason for my nervousness with the journey home was that in Emma's pre transplant days we knew her illness inside out. Her health was critical but we were au fait with all aspects of it and had grown into it with each progression of her illness. Now in her early post transplant days we were in completely new territory and I found this new responsibility very frightening. I was afraid that something would happen to her on the flight and I would not know how to help her.

When we got on to the plane a young girl sat down beside us. I believe that her sitting beside us was an answer to prayer as in the course of conversation we discovered that she was studying to be a pharmacist. She also had had some relations in her family who had had CF. We were talking so much that before we knew it we were landing in Dublin Airport.

The plane must have parked at the far end of the terminal building as we had quite a long walk before we reached the baggage reclaim area. It was a tough walk for Emma along the corridors because her legs and feet were still weak from the operation but also from her being wheelchair bound the previous year. I carried all our hand luggage and we stopped every so often at seats along the way so she could regain her strength before walking the next part of the way.

When we came through to the Arrivals, it was great to see my brother Alan there waiting for us. He had brought a very special surprise with him...Luke. It was great to see their smiling faces and to be back in Dublin.

It was a strange journey home to our house because in many ways everything was familiar now that we were back in Dublin but in many other ways I felt disconnected from it all.

When I walked into our home that night, the first thing that struck me was colours. I didn't realized how pale and bland our surroundings had been for the past six weeks with the main colour in the hospital being white. It was so good to sleep in the comfort of my own bed that night and to be back home.

18

The First Year Post-Transplant

One of the reasons for writing this essential chapter is to show that although the transplant was an amazing, life-changing milestone in our lives, it was not the end of us living with long term illness. It would be easy to look at our situation and say that everything is great and, without a shadow of a doubt, quality of life has been restored to us, but there has to be the balance of the acknowledgement of life post transplant and also the fact that Luke still needs a level of care for his CF and we do not know how his health will develop in future years.

Immediately after the transplant we were all in a stage of recovery not only from Emma's transplant experience but also from the years that went ahead of it. Particularly the 372 days before transplant when things had been very traumatic.

I was in a state of physical, emotional, mental and possibly spiritual burnout and I could not fully appreciate the new quality of life that we had.

In those early months post transplant I just wanted to go and live in a cottage in the remotest part of the country. I felt all I could cope with every day would be a short, quiet walk to the local grocery shop and basic housekeeping duties like making dinner for us all. Burnout is a horrible place to be. I felt like such a failure. I felt that I had handled our years of crisis the wrong way. I felt so disconnected from everything and everyone around me.

I valued my very wise friend's advice that I needed to talk to someone so I could debrief about the traumas we had been through pre and post transplant. I didn't know anyone who would understand the specifics of what we had faced and in my exhaustion I let this slide, I didn't follow through on finding someone. I think this is why it took me longer to rediscover my energy and motivation for life.

I felt Emma and Luke bounced back from the trauma quicker than I did and it frustrated me that I felt so disconnected from life.

I really needed complete rest but that was not possible. There was so much to be done. I felt like a failure to Emma and Luke. With God's help I had always been strong for them and I believed that strength, along with their faith, helped carry them through difficult times. Now I was so exhausted I felt I had nothing left to give. My resources were depleted.

We had been whisked out of our lives at a moment's notice and dropped back home 6 weeks later. In many ways it seemed like we were now living a different life as so many things had changed. In looking at the changes we faced I will start with the positives.

Emma's health was amazing…she could breathe with no oxygen assistance…there was no mucus to cough up, her new lungs did not have CF…no IV's needed because there were no infections present…she could walk because she had the breath and the energy…she could laugh without choking on mucus…she had so much energy…her appetite had returned. It was a miracle…a second chance at life…a new beginning…the best birthday present she could ever have.

We had visited the transplant co-ordinators in their office sometime during Emma's recovery. Being the curious people we are, we asked what Emma's old lungs would have looked like compared to her new lungs. Neil brought up some images on the computer screen. Wow, it was incredible.

The old lungs were scarred and had collapsed in parts, there were marks all over the x-ray images. On the computer image of the new lungs, it was like as if someone had wiped the slate clean. The lungs were perfect, healthy, and had no marks on them at all.

The new lungs meant Emma did not have CF on her lungs anymore but she still had CF in her digestion, CF osteoperosis and CF diabetes and all the treatment and care that came with each of these aspects of her health.

Her new medication regime included a nebuliser twice daily. She also had approximately 30 doses of medication to take during the day which included anti-rejection drugs which she would need to take for the rest of her life. She would have to take her temperature every day as it is important to detect rejection early so treatment can be started immediately.

Post transplant is an acute situation as regards infections. Although we were on a learning curve with Emma's new medication regime, it was more manageable compared to what we had been through before the transplant. We continued to be careful at home that Emma and Luke did not share things like towels, cutlery or drinking glasses as we had to minimise the risk of infection. The anti rejection drugs meant Emma was imuno suppressed so it would be extremely risky to her health to get an infection.

One of the major changes was that in the space of six weeks Emma had gone from being 24 hour care to taking on the responsibility for her new medication regime and also having a new energy for living. I found the change in my role as carer to be a huge readjustment. It was now a role of supporting her in her rehabilitation and accompanying her to hospital check ups here in Dublin and across in Newcastle in England. She had to return to Newcastle at intervals for a bronchoscopy to see if there was any rejection.

Even though Emma bounced back from her ordeal there was still physical recovery to be made. Simple things like walking upset her. Her feet were sore and her legs were weak.

She had so much energy compared to before but her body needed time to recover. Many times I had to remind her of how far she had come and had to encourage her to be patient with her recovery. She had been in a wheelchair for almost a year before the transplant and the muscles in her legs would need time to strengthen again. I also noticed that initially she got frustrated with doing everyday things. For the year previous every day her job was to breathe, nothing else was expected of her because her health was so poorly. Post transplant, however, all that changed. I often heard her let out a deep sign when she was trying to do everyday things that she had got out of the habit of doing.

With each deterioration of Emma's health, her role within the family had changed. It wasn't something that I thought about at the time, it just seemed to be highlighted post transplant when I saw the change in her as she started living her life again.

Before the transplant she struggled for every breath, after the transplant we had the sound of her singing in the house. It was a positive readjustment for us, but still it took a bit of getting used to that the silence which had descended on our home in the previous year was now being replaced with her singing. It was such a miracle that she now had the breath to sing.

I know the biggest adjustment post transplant was a psychological one. We had been totally prepared for Emma to die if the lungs did not come in time. Now we had to do a complete turnaround and learn to live again. We had been grieving for 372 days before Emma had her transplant and that process could not just be switched off. It would take time to readjust.

I was talking to Ger, our CF Nurse Specialist, one time about this. We agreed that as we are a spiritual family we had a bigger adjustment to make because we had accepted and were prepared for Emma dying. Whereas if we were in denial there would have been less of an adjustment to make post transplant

Emma had missed out on so much life and was now ready to catch up. She was keen to get back to school and her social life as soon as possible. She would have been going into 5th year in school but as her health had been so critical we had looked into home schooling.

I had finally got the energy for filling in the forms for this just before she was called for her transplant. We did consider it for a while after the transplant and even had the forms approved. By this stage Emma had been so keen to get back to school to see her friends that we did not need to avail of the home schooling. She returned to school two months after the transplant. She did half days at first and only took on the subjects she needed to do for her career choice. The teachers were excellent again in their care.

They wanted to make sure that she did not put herself under unnecessary pressure as they did not want her health to go downhill again. The school nurse was keen to hear all about our experiences with the transplant so we had a chat for about two hours. She remarked that with all my experience of nursing Emma and Luke over the years I could be a specialist because it's not just about qualifications but experience too. On Emma's first day back to school the teacher in the library told Emma to go to her if she needed anything…the school nurse sent an encouraging text…another teacher gave Emma a note so she could get out of class 5 minutes early to avoid the busy corridors. They really were brilliant in the way they looked out for her.

While we had been in Newcastle, I was very proud of the way Luke handled our circumstances. It was not easy for him to be left behind but he readjusted so well.

Luke's health continued to be good. He had really taken to the new physiotherapy device, Acapello, so in doing regular physio for an hour everyday this was keeping his lungs reasonably clear.

While I had been in Newcastle with Emma, Luke had the responsibility of doing his medicines and nebulizers every day. On my return, he continued to do his medication regime and so there was another readjustment in my role as carer. It was now a supportive role, accompanying him to hospital clinic visits, monthly port flushes, and liaising with the hospital about his care. Subsequent cough swabs showed up the major CF infections but thankfully these could be treated with oral antibiotics. Mostly he kept well, there were just some times that he had allergic reactions to medication some of which were quite severe.

It was a positive thing that Emma and Luke took on their medication regimes with mature and responsible attitudes. With this type of long term illness, there comes a point where the patient had to take on the responsibility of their medicines as it gives them more freedom and independence. Somewhere in the middle of all the intense health issues we had faced over the years I discovered that I was good at nursing and always rose to the challenge of learning about new medicines and administering treatments.

Post transplant with my changed carer's role, I felt redundant as my nursing skills were no longer needed to the same extent.

Another major readjustment post transplant was that our lives no longer revolved around hospitals and 24 hour care. While this is a positive improvement in our quality of life, I found this phase lonely. Before Emma's transplant, every day we were surrounded with the care and support of our hospital family and also the team from the oxygen company.

Post transplant I realized I was grieving for the loss of their daily presence in our lives.

The morning after we arrived home from Newcastle we started letting our friends know we were home. We had only told family and one or two friends we were coming home. Some of our neighbours had very kindly wanted to organise a welcoming party to greet us at the Airport but we did not feel up to this as we needed time to recover. Also Emma was to avoid crowded places to minimise the risk of infection.

I phoned my boss in work to let her know that I had arrived back in Dublin the previous night, Friday, at midnight and that I would be at work on Monday. I was on a high and bursting to tell everyone about our positive experiences during the transplant.

We went to Church on the Sunday morning. It was great to see our Church family again and they were all delighted to see Emma doing so well. We had left Dublin with Emma's days of living numbered and everyone was delighted to see Emma this side of transplant and recovery. There was a great buzz about the place and we were all so thankful for the positive outcome to the crisis we had been facing and that our prayers had been answered the way we hoped they would be.

The opportunity to talk about our experiences were slow in coming which was a bit frustrating as we were eager to talk about it. Gradually over the next while we got the chance to tell our story or part of our story in many places… church services…television services…magazines…newspaper articles…radio programmes…speaking to parents and womens groups…talking to a trauma class at a university. One of the ways our circumstances had changed me over the years is that I went from being painfully shy in even basic conversations to be completely at ease talking to groups.

I returned to work on the Monday after we were back in Dublin. The first day or two I had problems recognizing the currency and I had to take extra time to make sure I gave the customers the right change. I temporarily forgot my Chip and Pin number also. Many times over the next few months I almost handed in my notice because I was still so tired. In the year pre transplant that I had reduced my hours, so I could give Emma 24 hour care, the dynamics had changed in work with changes that had come from Head Office. Increasingly, the only hours available to me were afternoon hours but it was the morning hours that suited our family circumstances. Also my hours were at different times each day and I needed more routine than that. I did not have the energy to go looking for another job but I knew in time that I would have to look for a job that had regular and more suitable hours.

The traumas we had been through and the experience of living with only necessary basics for the six weeks left me with the feeling of wanting to tidy out our house when I came back home. It's not that we had a lot in the house, it's just that in my burnout I felt there was unnecessary clutter around the place. In the trauma we had faced I knew that after the basics such as a roof over our heads, food in our mouths and money to pay the bills, the next important things that mattered were friendships and people.

Many things in our house looked old like as if our lives had been on hold for three years and in many ways it had been as we daily devoted our time to critical health issues and basic survival.

Also the dynamics within the family had changed. While Emma was critically ill, if a sibling disagreement was brewing between Emma and Luke, I would always tell Luke to go easy on her as she was not well. Now, post transplant, they had to readjust to a more balanced brother/sister relationship and communication.

Pre transplant my life and Emma's life had blended into one because we spent so much time together as she needed all that extra care. If anyone asked how things were I answered as 'we' instead of 'I'.

Post transplant Emma and I had to learn to live our own lives again. This meant different things for each of us. For Emma, in the next few years, she would face her Leaving Certificate exams, possible College, a job and the opportunity to follow her dreams. Hopefully her health would keep well for all of this.

With all this potential freedom and independence for Emma, I was spending more time alone and found this readjustment hugely difficult at first.

THREE MONTHS POST TRANSPLANT

Emma's health continued to be reasonable so long as she kept up the daily meds and nebulizers. She needed to do regular daily exercise so she joined the gym. It was a bit of an eye opener to the girl who was filling in the health section on the gym Application Form. She said she would look after Emma's fitness programme as if anyone else read it they would not believe she had accepted Emma's application.

We reassured her that it was ok for Emma to be at the gym and gave her contact numbers so she could confirm it with the hospital physiotherapist.

We were beginning to see the fulfillment of the verse Emma had been given before her transplant…'For I know the plans I have for you, plans to prosper you and not to harm you, plans to give you hope and a future' Jeremiah 29 vs. 11

We had to be careful with her health as we did not want her lungs to reject. She was to go to Funderland with her friends but when we checked with the hospital they said she was not to do extreme sports for 6 months post transplant. So she went with her friends but could not go on any of the rides.

We had to return to Newcastle in December, 3 months after her transplant, for a bronchoscopy to see if there was any rejection. I was still only working 10 hours a week and to have the time off to go to Newcastle with Emma, I rearranged my working hours into two days. I did not want to go back to Newcastle. We had only come back home in mid October. I was not ready to be away from home again so soon.

We were in Newcastle for four days altogether and the result of the test was that there was no rejection. It was good to see everyone again and the local Minister and his wife very kindly asked us to stay at their house. It was like staying at a home away from home.

In the year pre transplant nothing had been demanded of Emma as she was so ill but now there was a huge psychological adjustment and she needed time to regain perspective.

It was a strange feeling at times to come across something, like one of her inhalers, which had been so necessary three months previously but was no longer needed.

I was asked if I would talk to the mother of a boy who was going for transplant and of course I agreed to so we could share our experience with them and help to answer any questions they had as they started into the process of transplant.

We held a Thanksgiving service just before Christmas and 80 of our friends were there to celebrate the miracle of Emma's transplant with us, to praise God and to thank Him for carrying us through the last few years.

We were heading towards Christmas at this stage and I was very much aware that although we were three months post transplant, the donor's family we only three months into their grieving and they were about to face their first Christmas without their child.

That year we had our first Christmas, in a long time, with no traumas. Sometimes over the Christmas I got flashbacks of nights when I had wheeled Emma into the hospital as an emergency because she could not breathe. Or I would get flashbacks of the hospital cubicle where we had spent so much time. Or sometimes familiar smells would bring back memories of our days in Newcastle.

Luke was keeping reasonably well as long as he continued his medication regime and physiotherapy daily.

I was still recovering from the exhaustion of the trauma of the past three years. I was okay when I was in the company of friends but when I was alone the emptiness engulfed me. I grieved for all the people who had been a daily part of our lives pre transplant and were not now since the transplant.

Sometimes when I was talking to people about Emma's recovery I could hear myself saying the words but they were echoing around my head and it was such an effort to say the words. Initially after coming back from the transplant I wanted to tell everyone about the positive experience we had had but as the weeks went on and I started dealing with all the emotions of what we had been through pre transplant, I felt deflated.

There is a Life Change chart which has a list of stressful life events and the points for each one. Depending on the total points, they give an indication of how they think this would affect your health. My total points for the pre transplant days was over 300.

This suggests that if the situation had continued I would run an 80% risk of illness within two years. Although my stress levels were dramatically reduced now, I still needed time to recover.

During the intensity of the previous years my prayer life and quiet time had suffered because I did not have the time and energy I would have wanted to spend on it. My relationship with God had changed and I knew I needed to begin working on getting this back on track because the closeness of my relationship with God was what kept me centered and gave me hope.

The night Emma had been called to Newcastle for transplant we had been escorted to Dublin Airport by three Garda on motorcycles. I wrote to the Sergeant two months after Emma's transplant to let them know how things worked out. I imagined that they often do escorts like that but would not necessarily know how things worked out. I wanted to tell them how she was in her recovery and also to thank them for getting us to the Airport safely and quickly that night. He was delighted to get my letter telling him how things turned out and he passed the good news to the two other Garda. He had called to our house two weeks after Emma's transplant to find out how things were but we were still in Newcastle at that time.

There were moments of realisation as well. I can still remember standing in a queue at a local supermarket and it suddenly stuck me that we had lived through 18 years of some of the most terrible life situations but with God's help we came through. That realisation changed my outlook for the future, I knew that we would be able to face whatever situations came our way just as we had done in the past. However I also acknowledged to myself that I did not want us to have to face any more difficult situations for a very long time.

•••

SIX MONTHS POST TRANSPLANT

Emma had missed out on usual friendships as her CF had taken up so much of her time over the years. There was quite a gap in communication now that she was trying to socialise more. I knew in time that would change. The more she socialized with her friends, the less of a gap there would be. It was difficult for her in these early days post transplant.

Emma continued to have no rejection in her lungs which was a real blessing. She was still in a time of recovery. Her feet were still sore to walk on. In time this would improve.

It was always a blessing to be asked to share part of our story through interviews or talks. Some positives were that Emma's PEG feeding tube was removed. It was a great relief to have it gone. Another positive was that Robbie from the oxygen company called 6 months after the transplant to collect Emma's oxygen compressor, Bipap machine and extra oxygen cylinders. Having these pieces of equipment out of the house meant less reminders of the trauma we had been through.

Also I was going through my mobile phone list of numbers and realized that I did not need ten of the hospital phone numbers anymore, so I deleted these. Sometimes it seems very unreal to have lived through the hell we had been through.

There was still a certain amount of after care needed including another trip to Newcastle for a bronchoscopy to see if there was any rejection. Again I did the same with my working hours. The boss kindly rearranged the work rota so I could do my 10 hours in two days and would then be free to accompany Emma to Newcastle. There was no rejection again.

Luke's health continued to be reasonable. He did have some unexpected tests, follow up treatment, routine tests, new medications, allergic reactions and aspects of his health had to be monitored. He was also dealing with the knowledge that

Emma had had her transplant but he had not so it was obviously on his mind about what the future may hold for him.

I was still getting flashbacks of what we had been through. In one of the flashbacks, Emma was standing over the sink, vomiting up mucus, crying because she could not breathe and telling me she could not go on like this. Her oxygen tube was linked up to her and she looked so frail.

I still struggled with low energy levels, lack of motivation, feeling lightheaded and had pains in my legs. We had had the emotional roller coasters, the adrenelin rushes, the intensity, the highs and then the lows as life plodded on with the readjustments post transplant. It sometimes felt like a mountain that could not be climbed. For every day that I had had watched Emma dying, something inside me died. I was not sure how to get that spark back. Was it gone forever? Did it come back with time? It seemed like it would never return but then I remembered a comment I had read somewhere years previous and wrote into my encouragement book…Never make permanent decisions based on temporary circumstances. This encouraged me to believe that in time things would sort themselves out.

A perfect day, at this time, would have been to be able to stay in bed for the whole day, curled up under my duvet. I had been given a Birthday present of a voucher for a massage at a local health health clinic. The day of my appointment, the weather was so cold outside and I noticed the snow up on the mountains. The girl who would give me the massage left me alone in a room so I could get ready and she would return shortly. I remember lying in a semi-darkened room, on the plinth with a duvet above me and feeling the heat of an electric blanket under me. Even if the girl did not return that would have been heaven to lie there for an hour and relax. However she did return and later leaving the health clinic having been pampered for that hour, I felt that my energy for life was beginning to return to me.

My prayers at this time were that God would inject some life back into me.

•••

NINE MONTHS POST TRANSPLANT

I had discovered earlier in my life that when things seemed out of control I did what I could to take control of the circumstances rather than being controlled by them. This way I coped better.

As I began to slowly feel the energy return to me now, I decided that I needed to make some changes. One of these was a change in job. I know I was good at nursing and caring for Emma and Luke all those years that we had been living with their illness and I wanted to find a job where I could use the wealth of experience I had built up over the years. I also enjoyed working with children so I started applying for jobs as a Special Needs Assistant within a primary school.

I was successful in getting a job as an SNA and looked forward to starting it at the beginning of the next school year.

We returned to Newcastle for Emma to have her bronchoscopy. She was admitted to the ward and would have the procedure the following day. When I said goodbye to her that night and she walked down the ward back to her room, I got flashbacks of when she had been critically ill in hospital and sometimes at night time she would walk up to the door of the ward with me to say goodnight. When our present situation reminded me of that I wanted to scoop her up in my arms and take her with me, not leave her in the hospital overnight.

We got the opportunity to go on holidays to France. We had a lovely time enjoying the good weather and the relaxing time. Unfortunately on our return it was discovered that Emma's lung function had dropped 30%. It could have been one or a combination of reasons that caused this. Thankfully when the hospital here in Dublin, which Emma attended since her transplant, suggested IV's I was allowed to do them at home so Emma did not have to stay in hospital. I administered the home IV's for a week and then in typical Emma get-up-and-go style, she went camping with friends. I had administered the morning dose of IV's at 7am and by midday she was at the meeting point with her friends.

After all the years of being held back by her illness I could not deny her the experience even though I worried about her health while camping out in a tent in the rain.

Eight months post transplant, there was a special Church service which Emma and Luke were involved in. That morning an idea came to me. I decided as the bubbles which I had previously bought were no longer needed I would use them for a happy occasion instead.

I made a list of those who I would give the bubbles to and when I counted how many people were on the list, this number matched the exact amount of bubbles I had. When I was giving these to family and friends I explained that the bubbles were initially bought for another reason but thankfully we were able to use them that day for a happier reason. Most people were tearful when I explained the story behind the bubbles to them.

For a while after the transplant I struggled with why God had allowed us to go through the hell of watching Emma die for a whole year before she was called for transplant.

Years previous to this I had bought some tapes by a woman who had a healing ministry. In one of the tapes when talking about bad times she poses the question…How do you come out of this time better not bitter? She suggests that after acknowledging the bad experience you have to say to God that although you don't understand why you had to go through it, you trust that He had a reason for allowing that to happen. I had come to the point that I was ready to do this because I was tired of questioning Him. I prayed something along these lines to God and then my spirit started to dance inside me. I felt so happy and relieved to be in a place of acceptance rather than questioning.

•••

THE SUMMER BEFORE EMMA WAS ONE YEAR POST TRANSPLANT

I was looking at my Bank statement and I saw the amount for the birthday food I had been buying for Emma earlier in the day that she was called for transplant. It momentarily brought me back to that day's events and how our lives were changed.

In August 2007 Emma had her final visit to Newcastle for her last bronchoscopy. It was sad having to say goodbye to all the team over there. The positive side was that we got to see all the people we would have wanted to say goodbye to. In the hospital corridor we met Chris, the surgeon who had performed Emma's transplant. He was delighted to see her looking so well. Dr. Gerry was no longer working at that particular hospital but he had heard we were over and came to say 'Hi'. It was great to see him as we had appreciated his positive attitude while we were over in Newcastle for Emma's life saving transplant. At Dublin airport we were amazed to see the girl who had been on the plane the night we had come home from Emma's transplant. She had now finished the course she had been doing back then and got her Diploma.

The further I got from those traumas we had been through, the more I was able to move on from the awfulness and choose to live again in the present.

I am forever changed by what we have been through. I feel I am calmer, less intense about life.

I had some more opportunities to share our story with women's groups and parent's groups. I am always amazed by how our story touches many people in different ways and encourages them to keep going in difficult times.

When Emma was critically ill we had applied for a parking permit which would allow us to park in a disabled spot. We had received this in the post just before Emma was called for transplant so we never got to use it. I returned it to the people who had supplied us with it and explained why I was returning it. They said the letter was a 'real bright spot in their day' when they heard the good news about Emma's health.

We were still going through some issues of readdressing the balances in family relationships and communication. The mother / daughter relationship between Emma and I had been very close during the time of her critical health but now we were in a time of readjustment to the normal type of mother / daughter relationship during teenage years.

•••

ONE YEAR POST TRANSPLANT

We had a party. We invited family and friends who had been so supportive during the crisis we had been through. It was great to have the room filled with the laughter and chat as everyone enjoyed themselves. The Saturday of the party was the actual day that her transplant had been on the year before. The donor's family were very much on my mind that day.

My faith was changed by what we had lived through. I had been through so much where the only answer was to pray and trust that my faith had changed to being more simple, more accepting. I had realised that often God does not remove the difficulties we face in life but He is with us through them, providing for us and caring for us. I know from my experience this filled me with an underlying peace which helped me face challenges with a different perspective.

I had changed also. I don't think I could have gone through the experiences of the last 18 years and not be changed. Everybody has their own idea of what life situation they consider to be awful but for me watching my daughter critically ill for 372 days had almost destroyed me. Having come through that gave me a different outlook on life.

As I am putting the finishing touches on this book, we are two years post transplant.Our story continues as we live with the daily challenges of long term illness but we are in a phase where neither of them are critically ill in hospital and their medications can be done daily at home. Their daily health regimes continue with medication, nebulisers and monitoring aspects of their health, also physiotherapy for Luke. They both have regular clinic visits at the different hospitals they attend. Sometimes there are unexpected treatments needed daily for short periods of time like when there is a severe allergic reaction or for a bone fracture (due to osteoporosis). At other times there are routine treatments needed for a couple of weeks. Many times recently I have been asked if Emma is completely healed. She still has CF osteoporosis, CF diabetes, CF in her digestion and is immuno suppressed. The transplant gave her back a quality of life that had eluded her for so long and was a life changing, positive milestone in our journey of living with long term illness. I admire Emma and Luke for the way they cope with the day to day intrusion that managing their illness brings to their lives and also for their positive attitudes of living life to the full. We don't know what the future holds as regards how Luke's health will progress over the years or how many years Emma has post transplant. We make the best of every day knowing that life is short and can change at a moment's notice.

We continue to live one day at a time and to know that our God who has faithfully cared for us in the past will continue to care for us whatever the future holds.